SUCCESSFUL
SMALL GARDENS

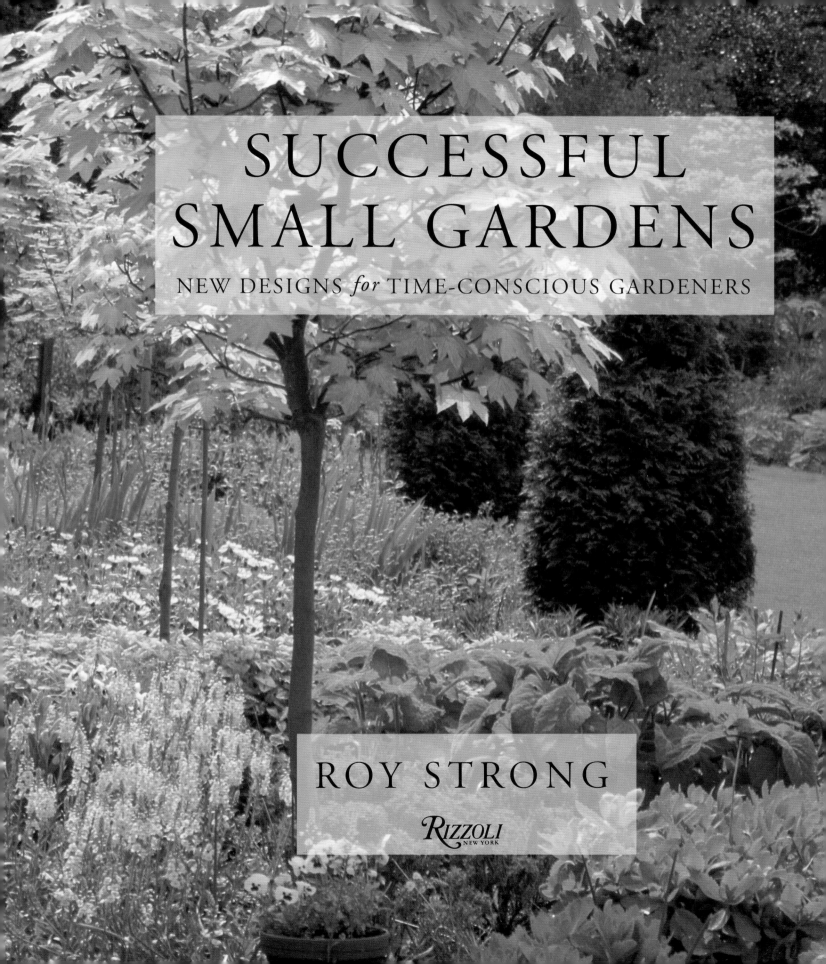

SUCCESSFUL SMALL GARDENS

NEW DESIGNS *for* TIME-CONSCIOUS GARDENERS

ROY STRONG

RIZZOLI
NEW YORK

This book is a tribute to the garden owners and designers whose work we have been able to include. Their gardens are evidence of the enormous vitality and variety in small garden-making today. I am grateful to all of them for letting us share in their achievement, as it has meant providing us with plans and planting details as well as responding to our many small queries. I am indebted to Prue Bucknall in our search to find a new way of presenting the information in this book to make it as clear as possible to the reader. In that search we have been hugely assisted by Joanna Logan's delightful but down-to-earth groundplans. Roy Strong

Endpapers Cushions of clipped box and santolina, both needing shearing annually, are in perfect harmony with the stone sculpture.

Page 1 Virginia creeper can transform a garden wall into a beacon of crimson when its leaves change colour in the autumn, but it requires hard winter pruning.

Pages 2-3 An avenue of standard maples underplanted with blocks of pale colour and backed by thuja topiary is deceptively elaborate: the trees need only annual attention, and the density of the planting beneath them acts as a weed-suppressor.

First published in the United States of America in 1995 by
RIZZOLI INTERNATIONAL PUBLICATIONS, INC.
300 Park Avenue South, New York, NY 10010

First published in Great Britain in 1994 by
CONRAN OCTOPUS LIMITED

First paperback edition published in 1999

ISBN 0-8478-2197-8

LC 94-67378

Printed in China

CONTENTS

Above and right Two informally planted areas in my garden at The Laskett, in Herefordshire, are given a feeling of firm structure by the large ornaments that provide year-round focal points. Drifts of flowers attendant on a statue of Flora (*above*) bring a succession of bloom from mid-winter to the late spring. They include snowdrops, crocuses, aconites, scillas, narcissi, fritillaries, miniature daffodils, tulips, chionodoxas and irises. The grass is not cut until late summer to allow the bulbs to multiply, and although the bulbs need topping up from time to time, the area requires very little attention. A small sheltered glade beneath birch and rowan trees (*right*) houses a collection of hellebores, primulas, cyclamen, miniature daffodils, sternbergia and crown imperials with drifts of hardy geraniums and pulmonaria. It flourishes in the spring and lies dormant while the trees are in leaf. This is a deceptively simple-looking area; it does, in fact demand regular doses of compost and summer weeding.

MAKING A GARDEN

A small garden is a vision which must be firmly rooted in practicality. This consists of your own interest in terms of time and money, on which depends the fulfilment of the design. Begin by defining your interest quite precisely, for it will determine the kind of garden you can have (although not, I hasten to add, its style, for virtually every option will be open to you). Other factors which affect choice are external: soil, aspect and climate, all of which must be taken into account. Armed with this information, you are ready to peruse the elements which have gone into the making of the gardens in this book. Although all very different in style, they share one thing in common: they are proven successes.

It is often assumed that a desire for low maintenance narrows your choice down to a very few options and that these actually amount to a style. This is not true. The first nine gardens for those hard-pressed for time demand only about an hour a week, yet they embrace virtually every garden effect from water to training, from topiary to herbaceous planting. Seven out of the twelve other gardens, for those who are either time-conscious or with time to spare, are adaptable for people with little time by the simple process of simplifying the planting. The reason that so many options are open with so little input is because of the importance attached throughout this book to the role of structure. It reminds us that historically gardening is a branch of architecture: it is about defining space in which people will move. By structure I mean the initial design elements embodied in hard built surfaces such as paths and ornaments or living ones such as grass and hedges. The more time and money spent on getting these right in the first place, the better your garden will be and the easier to maintain.

It is often assumed that structure is only relevant to formal styles. This again is not true. Informality, when its principles are analysed, calls for as much, if not more structure: it is simply not so immediately obvious. For each garden featured in this book the structure has been deliberately separated from the more general planting to reinforce its importance.

There is, however, a second general truth: the more built and plant structure you have, the fewer maintenance problems you will have.

Above and right My own garden, although large overall, is made up of a series of small, contrasting, gardens, each of which is a complete composition in its own right. This late spring view of the Rose Garden looking through to the Silver Jubilee Garden beyond (*above*) shows the firm structure of both gardens. The Rose Garden, held in by yew hedges, has a symmetrical pattern of box-edged beds planted with a mixture of spring-flowering tulips and perennials, neither requiring a great deal of maintenance. In summer the central circular bed is a froth of pale violet nepeta encircled by *Alchemilla mollis*, while the outer beds are filled with purple *Lavandula angustifolia* 'Hidcote' and rue. Four standard amelanchiers, four roses in the spandrels and a large urn provide the vertical accents.

Conversely, the more complex the planting, the greater will be the demand on your time. Hard surfaces such as stone, slabs, brick, setts and gravel, complemented by permanent plant features, like low box hedging or grass, mark out the ground pattern. Structures of stone, brick, metal or fibreglass – arches, statues, containers or pavilions – together with living structures, such as hedging or topiary, establish a garden's verticals.

Every design decision about your garden has such practical implications and these should be taken on board at the planning stage. A stone or brick path for example will need only sweeping and possibly an annual application of weedkiller. Gravel will call for raking plus weeding or weedkilling. A grass path will require almost weekly mowing during the season, but if you make the path the width of your mower it will be necessary to go down it only once. Similar upkeep

considerations apply when planting hedges. Privet, for example, will have to be cut several times in a season, whereas yew or box need be clipped only once.

Effort only really multiplies with elaboration in terms of planting. Some plants are inevitably more demanding than others. There are, for instance, specific clematis and roses which do not require any pruning, while others have to be pruned annually at particular seasons. Containers may have to be emptied and filled and planted up several times a year. The lesson is to select plants that reflect your ability to cope with them. Never buy or sow any before taking on board all they will demand in terms of attention, as well as whether they suit your soil, climate and the aspect.

One final word. When it comes to gardening a Scrooge-like mentality seems to seize people. It is essential to grasp that long-term ease

Above Looking back through the Silver Jubilee Garden into the Rose Garden in winter, demonstrates the crucial importance of structural planting and ornament in the creation of year-round garden interest. Devoid of seasonal flowers, the composition of clipped beech, yew and box with a considered placing of hard-surface elements makes the garden a theatre for the play of light throughout the winter months.

of maintenance is a fair return for what may seem initially a heavy financial outlay. Modern machinery such as petrol-driven shears, strimmers and mowers make easy what were once tedious, time-consuming chores. A sprinkler system with a timer will solve almost every watering problem at one blow. Do not stint on such things, nor on good-quality built and plant structure. If working out basic structure daunts you, there is much to be said for employing a professional garden designer who will bring a great deal of expert know-how to tailoring a garden to your level of commitment. That again is a worth-while investment. Use this collection of designs to indicate your preferences and aspirations. In the main, however, this selection has been assembled for those who, although they may use a professional builder for some of the structure, will, by and large, make their gardens themselves both for the economy and the enjoyment of doing so.

Left The parterre in the Yew Garden at The Laskett is planted with crown imperials and tulips for the spring. The beds are left bare during summer; the pattern made by the box hedging and the stone basket of fruit provides enough interest. The box and yew call for an annual clip and the bulbs, if fed with bonemeal, will last up to five years so that, apart from the lawn-mowing, this is a surprisingly easy area to maintain.

Above The Fountain Court at The Laskett is another example of the importance of structural planting and ornament. Irish yew and statues provide year-round vertical accents that need no attention, the beech hedges and box domes need an annual clip, and the rosemary screens beds filled with ground-cover plants. The fountain is turned off and baled out at the first frost.

GARDENS
for the
HARD-PRESSED

Previous pages A parterre is a surprisingly stylish low-maintenance solution for a tiny garden, once it is established, calling only for annual clipping and feeding. Here the dwarf box is shaped in an exciting contemporary idiom. The parterre is framed by a gravel path which needs occasional raking and perhaps annual weedkilling. The surrounding narrow beds are filled with low-maintenance plants; including a bold display of *Hydrangea macrophylla* and on the other side by a seat flanked by Solomon's seal and bergenia. A hornbeam hedge (also clipped annually) conceals a side passage with arches of jasmine.

Left A deeply satisfying garden in a cool, shady corner is made by texturally contrasting hard elements – the curving sculpted finial, the asymmetrical random stone walling and the regular geometry of the setts. These frame the tiny 'lawn' of baby's tears (*Soleirolia soleirolii*). Pots provide structure and interest even when empty; the flowers could vary with the seasons or from year to year.

Right The chief delight of this tiny but highly sophisticated garden of silvery grey plants lies in the subtly contrasting variations of colour, leaf shape and habit. They include santolina, rosemary, *Salvia nipponica officinalis* Purpurascens Group, *Phlomis fruticosa*, *Helichrysum lanatum*, artemisia, thyme and lavender. Although many do best in a sunny, sheltered site, they retain their leaves throughout the year and will go on for several years calling only for annual cutting back before they need replacing by new plants easily struck from cuttings.

Some of the most stylish of all gardens are in fact labour-saving. The nine included here call for only about an hour or so a week, plus a couple of annual blitzes in spring and autumn when major tasks such as pruning need to be done. They are also some of the most sophisticated and understated, because their design is founded on year-round built and evergreen structure rather than time-consuming planting schemes that vary with the seasons. There are few more elegant forms, for example, than the parterre and yet, once established, it calls only for an annual clip. Or, to take a contrasting style, naturalized bulbs provide a stunning garden picture which, with clever planting, will provide a continuous sequence of flower from late winter through spring till early summer. All that the bulbs require is careful planting in grass which should not be cut until late summer.

The more hard-surface structures you have, the easier the upkeep will be. These include paths, walls, balustrading, steps, urns and finials, obelisks and statues, arbours and pavilions. Their drawback is the initial cost, but that should be offset against the time saved in the long run, and their great advantage is the strength and immediacy of their effect. Built structures come in a wide range of materials: they can be of stone or reconstituted stone; or of wood, metal, or fibreglass (that can also simulate bronze), all of which bring other possibilities, especially in terms of colour and paint finishes. Avoid, if you can, cheap concrete and plastic. If these have to be used, site them where the eye will not dwell on them or where planting will conceal them. For the most conspicuous items do not stint on buying beautiful materials – old mellow brick, stone and reconstituted stone, cobbles and setts – as you will be looking at them the whole year round.

Left and right The same garden in early summer and autumn presents two very different but striking pictures. The basic structure is easily cared for. Brick and stone paths define a symmetrical group of box-hedged beds filled with a permanent planting of low maintenance weed-suppressors. The frothy lime-coloured flowerheads of *Alchemilla mollis* match the buds and young leaves of *Hydrangea macrophylla*. In their summer glory the hydrangea flowerheads make a luxuriant display of dusty pink – and the colour is echoed by the seat; all through the winter they will stay on the leafless stems, providing a still-life of dried flowers in bronze-brown. The cornucopia effect of the massed hydrangeas almost bursting the bounds of their confining box edging and dwarfing the acorn finial makes an interesting change from the conventional parterre where everything is neat and well defined.

The best structural planting for hedges is yew or box, both evergreen and with dense growth. If you can afford large plants, the effect will be virtually instant (although if nurtured, both grow far quicker than is supposed). Beech and hornbeam are also possibilities, for they also only require an annual cut. For vertical accents, choose small trees such as amelanchiers that will not call for annual pruning; some of the

Those fortunate enough to be making a garden in a damp woodland area can create a moss garden reminiscent of the ones in Japan. All that has to be done is to clear the scrub and allow the moss to grow and thicken. The main annual chore is to keep it clear of fallen leaves; and brushing with a stiff brush from time to time will keep the moss lawn in good trim. Here the wooded area is given articulation by a winding gravel path and an enclosing hedge, while the downy surface of the moss serves as an exhibition arena for contemporary art works. You can create a woodland by planting a group of tall saplings. Choose species with good bark such as maples and birches. Instead of encouraging moss, you could underplant the trees with bulbs.

prunus or crataegus give not only spring flowers but autumn fruits. For accents that are evergreen look towards fastigiate yew and certain of the cypresses and junipers with narrow and columnar growth. Then choose climbers to clothe man-made verticals. Look for species which require the minimum pruning and which will not ramp. Check their flowering season and aim for a sequence of bloom through as much of the year as possible.

Then embark on the infill planting. Look for shrubs which will not require much pruning and have both flowers and fruit or have a long flowering season as well as good foliage colour. Move on next to select perennials which rarely, if ever, call for lifting and dividing, and ground-cover plants. Careful research and planning at this stage will save countless hours in the garden later on.

Preparation of the soil is fundamental as it will reduce the weeds and ensure healthy plants. A weedkilling treatment may be necessary to eradicate infestations of perennial weeds before you embark on new planting. The soil must be annually dressed with fertilizer and compost. Mulching with things like wood chippings is a recent garden abomination; its labour-saving purpose can be achieved through either ground-cover plants or dense planting.

Remember that in a small garden one important feature will hold the entire composition together. Avoid being fussy and go for a single large statue, urn, finial or arbour. In a single gesture your garden will acquire instant identity. The rest should follow it, but beware, above all, the blandishments of the garden centres. They will tempt you to buy what you have not the time to care for or cultivate.

An informal garden, or area within a garden, can be made to give extra value by planting deciduous trees that have both spring and autumn interest, and underplanting them with bulbs or shade-loving plants. Bird cherry (*Prunus padus*) is a deciduous spreading tree with spikes of white flowers in late spring and small black fruits in late summer. The lilac beneath makes a pretty spring picture. Lilac is perhaps a luxury in a small garden because its glorious flowering season is short, but for many its scent makes it worth it. The delightful underplanting of narcissi will multiply if the grass is left uncut until mid-summer. The inclusion of both earlier and later bulbs would produce a succession of flower from mid-winter till late spring.

Above Permanent low-maintenance planting need not be dull. A carefully orchestrated planting of heathers can make a striking ground-cover garden in a site where the soil is on the acid side. Coming in a huge variety of foliage tints from darkest green to sulphur yellow, and with tiny flowers ranging from white through every shade of pink to deepest purple, heather calls only for annual shearing after flowering. Here heathers have been inset into good structure. A flight of steps is flanked by pairs of slow-growing conifers including thuja and *Chamaecyparis lawsoniana* 'Ellwoodii'. A terracotta pot flanked by hydrangeas forms a tableau at the close of the vista. The tapestry of cherry laurel and *Lonicera nitida* that forms the backdrop needs an annual clipping, and the ivy and hart's-tongue ferns colonizing the steps need a periodic tidy-up.

Right Choose plants that will enjoy not only your soil type but the aspect of the beds where you plant them. This path of setts winding through the green world of a shrubbery is bordered by lower-growing plants that make a ground cover full of textural contrast. Height on the sunnier side (to the left) is provided by mahonia, oak-leaved hydrangea and a viburnum. The pale-outlined foliage of *Fuchsia magellanica gracilis* 'Variegata' is echoed at ground level by a variegated ivy. On the shadier side the variegated theme is taken up by a mound of *Hosta fortunei* 'Albomarginata' and the smaller leaves of shrubby *Pieris japonica* 'Variegata'. Heart-shaped leaves of epimedium and a mossy carpet of *Soleirolia soleirolii* are interspersed with a variety of glossy-foliaged plants. The palmate leaves of *Fatsia japonica* deepen the shade below.

Left The shape of the paving echoes both the straight lines of the room within and the courtyard without, and the small sized slabs help to make the garden seem larger than it is. To the left, facing south, are the sun-loving plants, rosemary, santolina and roses. To the right a small but elegant specimen tree, *Gleditsia triacanthos* 'Sunburst', arises from a halo of ivy. The drifts of *Erigeron karvinskianus*, mostly self-sown between the bricks, are a master touch.

Right This tiny garden offers a really superb solution for a modern house. It deliberately accentuates the juxtaposition of two rectangular spaces, one indoor and one outdoor, and then treats their design in two contrasting but complementary styles. The softness that is usually provided by the interior in extensive use of fabrics is here left to the foliage outside.

A WILD COURTYARD GARDEN

Nostalgic gardens are apt to sit very uneasily with late twentieth-century architecture, which seems to call for a style of its own age. Here the artful disorder of the paved garden forms a surprising but wholly appropriate contrast to the clean-cut lines of the contemporary interior from where it is viewed. The effect is of two rooms, separated by a wall of glass that can be slid to one side in warm summers.

Well built walls, high enough not to be looked over, are essential to the success of this scheme: they give it the atmosphere of a private, if outdoor room. Good quality paving is also important. Neither material is cheap, but after this initial extravagant expenditure, the planting is positively inexpensive. Climbers clad the walls, and this backcloth is used for a sparing but considered planting of flowering

shrubs, roses and ground-cover plants with one choice small tree and a tiny herb bed at the centre.

Unlike most gardens this one never sets out to confuse its contours. That is its secret. There is a profusion of branch and foliage, but one is constantly aware that everything is held in by a firm containing rectangle that echoes the dining room. Although the garden presents, at first glance, a scene of calculated confusion, it is in fact quite the reverse. The simplicity of the design elements and the permanent nature of most of the planting mean that very little maintenance is required. Apart from winter and spring pruning and autumn cutting back, this outdoor room – like an indoor one – needs only generally tidying up: dead-heading, some clipping and gentle weeding.

THE STRUCTURE

The courtyard is 6 x 10 m/ 20 x 30 ft with brick walls of about 2.2 m/8 ft on all three sides. It is essential to ensure a free flow between the outside and the inside room, so that ideally the paving should be on the same level as the floor of the room, and the dividing window should be as unobtrusive as possible. The main view from the window is kept clear, apart from a small bed of low-growing herbs, and the border against the far wall is very narrow, ensuring as much sense of distance as possible.

BEDS AND BORDERS

Apart from the borders which line the three enclosing walls, there are two small beds let into the brick paving. One is a tiny herb bed, emphasized by a low clipped hedge on three sides of it. The other supports the small tree and a ground-cover of ivy but its edges have been obscured by the encroaching ivy from the south wall and border.

PAVING

The ground surface has been treated uniformly both in terms of colour and size; the introduction of mixtures of materials or pattern of any kind would upset the sense of ordered balance and unity of space that is so important, especially as it acts as a striking counterfoil to the range of texture and colour of the encroaching foliage. The choice of these frost-

resistant bricks was made because they do not attract lichen and therefore do not become treacherously slippery during wet weather. They were laid over a firm hard core base, and then a mixture of sand and compost was brushed into the crevices. These are now host to an increasing number of ground-hugging plants that soften the hard look of the bricks.

THE PLANTING

The most striking feature of the planting is the extensive use, on the shady areas of the walls, of *Hedera helix* 'Angularis Aurea', which has bright glossy green leaves streaked and splashed with butter-yellow. The result is a leafy tapestry of green and gold that lightens up what would otherwise be dark corners. This also gives the garden its background winter coat, for apart from the architectural leaves of the fatsia and the bergenia, most of the planting is geared towards providing a sequence of bloom running from spring to autumn. The workload is minimal: after the rampant ivy has been severely pruned back in the spring, there is just some cutting back, especially of the low teucrium hedge, dead-heading, occasional weeding and, of course, watering in dry weather, before the main autumn tidying up, and the winter pruning of the vines.

NORTH WALL AND BORDER

1 *Vitis vinifera* "Fragola' and *Actinidia deliciosa* clothe the wall.
2 The south-facing border is filled with soft-coloured and contrasting plants: *Rosmarinus* 'Miss Jessopp's Upright', *Helichrysum italicum*, *Hydrangea aspera* Villosa Group, *Rosa* 'Penelope', *Rosa* x *odorata* "Mutabilis', and *Rudbeckia fulgida deamii* with low-growing *Alchemilla mollis* and *Armeria maritima*.

EAST WALL AND BORDER

3 *Jasminum officinale* and *Abutilon* x *suntense* grow against the wall in the sunniest corner.
4 *Clematis montana* adds spring colour to the background of *Hedera helix* 'Angularis Aurea'.
5 *Rosa* 'Alister Stella Gray', *Brunnera macrophylla* 'Hadspen Cream', the white-streaked spears of *Iris pallida pallida* and the large glossy leaves of *Bergenia* Ballawley hybrids make up the border.

SOUTH WALL AND BORDER

6 The *Hedera helix* that clothes the wall also spills over into the border, making good ground cover around the bole of the garden's single tree.
7 *Gleditsia triacanthos* 'Sunburst'.
8 A big pot of *Fatsia japonica*.
9 A drift of *Macleaya microcarpa* 'Kelway's Coral Plume' grows in the corner.

HERB BED

10 A small range of herbs is contained in a bed

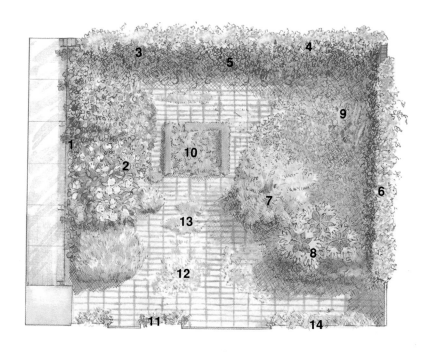

which has, on three sides, a low hedge of clipped *Teucrium* x *lucidrys*. The evergreen hedge needs clipping two or three times in the growing season to keep it in control, but as it is not integral to the design of the garden as a whole, it could be dispensed with.

HOUSE WALLS

11 *Jasminum officinale* adds summer scent round the large windows.

PAVING

12 The small cracks between the bricks have been colonized chiefly by self-seeded *Erigeron karvinskianus* which needs to be sheared back in the autumn.
13 Origanum grows in the sunnier areas.
14 *Soleirolia soleirolii* has taken over the shady corner beneath the house wall.

Below *Rosa* 'Penelope', a Hybrid Musk rose with vigorous growth and recurrent flowering.

A PERIOD PARTERRE GARDEN

Right The view from an upstairs window, looking down on the pattern below, is an additional pleasure. Symmetry of this kind gives a sense of order and tranquillity, while any feeling of rigidity is dispelled by the luxuriant planting frothing from the boundary walls, the pots of flowers, and the relaxed atmosphere of the sunny patio with its bench, table and chairs for alfresco living.

Left Winter is always the great test of a good garden. Here, under snow, the parterre looks magnificent, its curvilinear shapes emphasized to advantage. Notice how both the side walls have posts with linking cross members to support the planting.

The formal parterre, one of the great classics of garden design, is undergoing a renaissance today. Its effect is immediate from the moment of planting, and it is also, apart from the clipping required, labour-saving. At the back of this town house in Holland, two contrasting shades of gravel provide a dramatic foil to bold baroque scrollwork in glossy green box, while handsome fastigiate yew provides dark columns to emphasize the small but stately vista. This is a supremely elegant solution to an urban back garden site.

The parterre uses the rhythms of the seventeenth century, a golden age in Holland for the art of gardening. This is an appropriate style for an old town house, but just as the design of the parterre itself can be adapted – as here – to the smallest of sites, so a more contemporary design could easily be introduced for a more modern house.

Two thirds of the garden site are given over to the parterre, which provides a year-round evergreen pattern. Flowers in containers enliven the garden during the summer, and the boundary walls are softened by climbers and trained apple trees. The end third has been made into a sunny patio contained by hedges and with a delightful small pond and fountain as a focal point. The garden calls for little more than a couple of hours a week during the growing season to maintain it in top order. The only major undertaking is clipping the box, which needs to be carried out with precision once or twice a year.

THE STRUCTURE

Steps lead down from the house to a long narrow plot of about 33 x 6.5 m/ 110 x 21 ft. The central path is flanked by box hedges and mirror-image scrollwork parterres. A patio enclosure with a pond and a small fountain terminates the vista.

GRAVEL

Stone chippings and gravels come in a wide variety of colours, and the contrast between red and pale cream has been used in this garden to great effect to define the layout. The pale gravel of the path continued into the broader patio cleverly links the whole design.

SCROLLWORK

The box hedges along the path are some 30 cm/12 in high; the curving pattern is cut slightly lower. Because there is no planting inside the parterre, it is easy to lay plastic sheets on either side of the hedges to prevent trimmings falling on the gravel.

THE PLANTING

Box is the ideal plant for low hedging of this kind as it is frost hardy, can be clipped hard to keep it in shape, and is evergreen. *Santolina chamaecyparissus nana* or *Teucrium* x *lucidrys* are other possibilities, although not as satisfactory. For a parterre on a larger scale, *Lonicera nitida* or euonymus might be used. Dwarf box requires clipping in late spring or early summer, and sometimes again in late summer.

PARTERRE

1 Scrollwork and hedging are of the small-leaved *Buxus sempervirens* 'Suffruticosa'. An interesting variation would be to use golden box, *B.s.* 'Latifolia Maculata', for the scrollwork.
2 The fastigiate Irish yews (*Taxus baccata* 'Fastigiata') that have been used as the vertical accents will outgrow this tiny space within fifteen years; the grey-green *Juniperus communis* 'Hibernica' or the very narrow *J. scopulorum* 'Skyrocket' are slower growers and more easily clipped.
3 Containers add colour in summer: Shasta daisies (*Leucanthemum* x *superbum*) line the path, with blue and white agapanthus varieties

beside the steps.
4 The north-facing wall has espalier apples and *Hydrangea anomala petiolaris* against it.
5 The south-facing wall has more trained apples. Both walls have a creeping ground-cover of ivy at their feet.
6 There is a quince (*Cydonia oblonga*) in the corner near the patio.

PATIO GARDEN

7 A clipped hedge encloses the patio area.
8 A weeping laburnum hangs over a statue.
9 Two false acacias (*Robinia pseudoacacia*) in containers flank the central seat. These will need heavy annual pruning.
10 The borders behind the hedge are filled with lavender and planted with four standard *Rosa* 'Snow White'. In severe winters these have to be wrapped for protection.
11 The north-facing bed is lined with lavender, and planted with *Rosa* 'Belle de Tuylers', while *R.* 'Gloire de Dijon' climbs on the wall behind.
12 The south-facing wall supports another quince.
13 The pond has a planting of waterlilies and *Iris* 'Brown Cigar'.
14 Pots of evergreens and flowering plants such as white agapanthus are moved in and out of the area during the seasons.

FRONT GARDEN PARTERRES

Parterres can provide stylish solutions to all kinds of odd-shaped areas. Here a geometric arrangement of clipped box with an aerial screen of pleached limes makes an elegant front garden out of an awkward L-shaped site, one side of which is extremely narrow.

The effect of this garden would be instantaneous from the moment of planting, and even starting with small plants the parterre would be fully formed in five to eight years. This is a year-round garden dependent for its effect on lustrous greens and the architectural and sculptural qualities of the clipped hedges and trained trees. Both are responsive to the play of light at different times of day and throughout the year. Maintenance would consist of clipping the box twice a year – a lengthy but not particularly arduous procedure – pleaching the limes until they are established, and then pruning them in winter, as well as giving them an annual feed of bonemeal.

A cool garden like this one provides a perfect foil to the architecture, especially of warm red brick. It could also be deliberately planted as a contrast to a far more informal flower garden at the back of the house. The formula used here suits the eighteenth-century house, but a parterre would not look out of place in front of a contemporary building, providing its design reflected that of the architecture. Being placed so close to the house, the pleached limes will inevitably make the house darker, and are best suited to a warm, sunny climate. An alternative would be to fill the parterres with flowers.

THE STRUCTURE

The corner site is designed in two sections, in effect as two slightly different front gardens. The narrow strip of about 2 m/7 ft wide in front of the house is filled with a repeat pattern in box, the semi-circles at the front encompassing the trunks of an aerial hedge of pleached limes, and those at the back containing box cones.

PICKET FENCE

The delightful white picket fence adds greatly to the crispness of this composition, providing both contrast and enclosure. Such fences can be custom-built, but several types are now available commercially. Ideally they should reflect the character of the architectural detail – the window frames and doorcases – on the house. The openness of the fence allows light on to the box and also deflects the eye from the confined nature of the space behind.

PLEACHED LIMES

Limes (*Tilia platyphyllos* 'Rubra') are fast-growing and resilient to pruning, and within five years can achieve a good pleached appearance. Early training is best achieved by erecting a temporary framework of strong wires or canes to which branches and eventually the leader can be tied. This, and the pruning back and tying in of side shoots in winter, will require ladders or a mobile platform. The ultimate height of the aerial hedge will be determined by the position and the scale of its surroundings.

PARTERRE PATTERN

Careful consideration has been given here not only to the narrow space but also to the relationship of the design to the façade of the house: the limes, for example, are positioned precisely between the windows, and the solid simplicity of the planting matches that of the architectural detail. In a narrow space such as this, it is especially important to keep the design simple and unfussy. The symmetry is illusory, for the strip is wider at one end than the other. Clipped box balls run down the centre, and a different design on the corner of the house links both gardens, with an urn as a focal point. The wider area at the side of the house has room for a classic parterre design, with symmetrical beds and vases. A design like this one could be used for a larger front garden by making a mirror-image of the pattern on either side of a central garden path.

THE PLANTING

The basic planting is dwarf box (*Buxus sempervirens* 'Suffruticosa'), but other larger-leaved varieties could be used for the topiary specimens. The initial cost would be high if large plants and trained topiary specimens were purchased, but it does not take long to create a substantial hedge from smaller plants, while creating one's own topiary specimens brings a rare sense of horticultural achievement. Yew (*Taxus baccata*), or golden box (*Buxus sempervirens* 'Latifolia Maculata') would be equally successful for the topiary balls and cones, and *Ilex* x *altaclerensis* ' Golden King' would be stunning. A row of small decorative trees, such as amelanchier, malus or crataegus, pruned as mopheads would be a pretty alternative to the pleached limes if screening for privacy was not a priority. They would allow more light and would provide blossom in spring and fruit in autumn.

Right This view along the front of the house shows the pretty white picket fence and the pivotal vase; the garden chiefly depends for its success, however, on the sculptural effect of the clipped box.

Left The view from the balcony steps shows the extremely simple yet effective treatment of a space enclosed by high walls. The treillage acts as a strong architectural frame for the shrubbery of evergreens chosen carefully to ensure good foliage contrasts.

Right The balcony and steps are festooned with Virginia creeper (*Parthenocissus quinquefolia*) and clematis whose small leaves are good foil for the bold foliage of the *Acanthus mollis* underplanted with ivy below.

This tranquil oasis of green in the middle of a bustling capital would lift the spirits on the darkest day. The architecture of many inner cities produces all sorts of unsatisfactory sites for garden-making, often spaces – like this one – hemmed in on virtually every side with tall walls forming a gloomy uninviting well. Yet, with careful planning and skilful planting, such a restricted area can be transformed.

The solution in this instance has been to make the space into a courtyard terrace with a small pool as its focal point which reflects light and is itself enlivened by a modest fountain, pale coloured pea gravel which attracts yet more luminosity and a handsome small tree chosen for the brightness of its lime-green leaves. The fine mesh trellis on all four containing walls contributes an essential element to the scene, bestowing unity and, at the same time, breaking up and having a softening effect on the large expanses of rendered wall.

This is a garden which could more or less look after itself, particularly if it had a computerized watering system; it calls for little more than regular pruning of the shrubs, the addition of compost to the soil and a once-yearly planting of a few bedding plants. The planting is made up of a backbone of robust, reliable favourites such as box, laurel and hebes that are guaranteed to give year-round value, with seasonal in-filling of well-tried summer-flowering plants such as impatiens. Once established, a garden like this will go on for years providing an inviting place to sit and take the air.

AN ENCLOSED URBAN OASIS

THE STRUCTURE

The area here is square, 10 x 10 m/34 x 34 ft, and has been given a strong sense of underlying order by placing the circular pond at the visual centre of the garden, at the crossing of two axes leading from the balcony steps and from one of the house windows. In such a confined space, the simplicity of the scheme is the key to its success. Its essential 'softness' – a combination of lush, evergreen planting and a gravel 'carpet' – offsets the hardness of the built environment in which it is set. It is given cohesion by its continuous framework of trellis, by the smooth gravel, and by the extremely limited colour range of the plants.

POND (*below*)
The shallow raised pond is the garden's main focal point. A modest jet, driven by an electric pump controlled from the house, adds movement and sound, but an ornament would be an attractive alternative. The rim of the pond is almost wholly concealed by ivy; two pots of clipped box that flank the gap in the circle add interest.

GRAVEL
Gravel is an advantage in cities as it can be raked or even bleached to remove atmospheric pollution. Gravel works particularly well with a casual planting scheme that has no hard edges. Although paving would be easier to keep tidy, it would be less satisfying texturally and any ground-level pattern or geometry would be totally at variance with the scheme. Grass would simply not grow in these conditions.

TREILLAGE

Trellis provides the unifying feature of the enclosure, its effect strengthened by the foil of the pale walls. The deep, glossy green of the trellis helps to make the walls seem farther away and the cream background lightens the space and enhances the green foliage. The formula is easily adapted to any small site as long as its deceptive symmetry is preserved. Because the space is so confined, choose the simplest trellis to maintain the soothing atmosphere and keep the emphasis on the plants and pond. In a larger space it would be possible to make a more complex architectural composition of treillage arches and windows, pilasters and pediments. It is worth investing in the best, most durable quality so that by the time the trellis or walls behind it need repainting, the ivy will have grown sufficiently well to cover the blemishes.

PLANTING

The planting is virtually entirely of shade-tolerant shrubs that provide a year-round background of soothing greens occasionally flecked with a few blooms. Early spring brings scented mahonia flowers and the bright young foliage of the pieris. This is followed by the camellia and rhododendron flowers and then a sprinkling of summer bedding and, in the autumn, with the blazing crimson of the Virginia creeper on the balcony balustrade. A handful of early spring-flowering bulbs would be easy to tuck in among the shrubs, but strident summer colour would ruin the effect of tranquillity. The undefined shape of the border and the informality of the planting makes an appealing contrast to the necessarily rigid boundaries of the garden and the strictly circular pond. An atmospheric pollution-resistant ground-cover of ivy softens most of the lines; but there is always a danger of its encroaching too far. Indeed most of the work in the garden is concerned with control – pruning and clipping-back, and picking up fallen leaves and petals – but with so small an area, this would take very little time.

IVY

1 Being shade- and pollution-tolerant, ivy has been used extensively. It has been planted to scramble up the treillage,

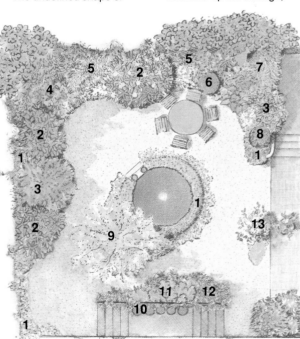

Above Pieris japonica, a shade-tolerant evergreen shrub, is noted for the colour of its spring foliage.

over the pond coping and as ground cover. Once established, it needs little attention except to curb its invasive tendencies and check its vigorous growth. *Hedera helix* has a range of decorative cultivars, with gold, white, grey or slightly pink markings, which could be used for a different overall effect.

BORDERS

These are partly shadowed by a chestnut tree and contain a mixed planting chiefly of shrubs that have been chosen for their shade tolerance and for the variety of their foliage.
2 *Rhododendron* variety.
3 *Choisya ternata.*
4 *Mahonia japonica.*
5 *Pieris japonica.*
6 *Buxus sempervirens.*
7 *Prunus laurocerasus.*

8 *Hebe* variety.
The foreground is filled with hosta varieties, and ground-covering ivy, while impatiens are added for summer-long flowers.

POOL AREA

9 *Gleditsia triacanthos* 'Sunburst' is a small, deciduous tree with delightful fernlike foliage that is golden yellow in spring changing to deep green in summer. An alternative choice might have been a prunus or malus that would give spring blossom and autumn fruit as well as autumn leaf colouring.

STEPS AND BALUSTRADE

10 Box balls in pots.
11 *Acanthus mollis.*
12 *Parthenocissus quinquefolia.*
13 *Pittosporum tenuifolium.*

A PERGOLA BACK GARDEN

-This ravishing inner city garden has been created in a tiny, unprepossessing space. It is a rare example of the marriage of initial low costs to subsequent low maintenance. It seems to recall the exuberant patio gardens of Spain whose essence is to be hidden, enclosed, tiled, to have a small water feature and be vibrant with foliage and flowers ranging from climbers to container plants. Here the concept has been transported to colder climes and clothed with a planting that recalls the romantic traditions of English country gardens.

The planting has been superimposed upon what is a strong asymmetrical structure dominated by the generously-proportioned pergola of painted wood. Tiles, marble chippings and concrete slabs frame a terrace for sitting out, a substantial mixed border and two small ponds – one with a fountain – that bring water, movement and reflected light to the garden. As the space available at ground level is so limited, full use has been made of every vertical surface, the amount of which has been extended by a pergola and by trellis on the containing walls which support an explosion of overhead bloom.

There is nothing in the construction of this garden beyond the capabilities of the competent home handyman, although the installation of the water features requires considerable care. Apart from the containers, which are welcome but dispensable, this is a very low maintenance garden calling for no more than about an hour a week in season, with annual autumn and spring blitzes. There is no lawn to mow and only one major bed to keep weeded. The most demanding elements are the ponds and fountain which need regular servicing, and the roses which need dead-heading, pruning and tying-in. The input, however, is minimal in return for such a flower-filled bower.

Above Viburnum tinus and pink *Rosa* 'Gloire de Guilan' grow below creamy-white *Rosa* 'Rambling Rector' on the left. On the right is a collection of grey foliage plants including santolina and artemisia and beyond is a glimpse of blue *Iris laevigata* arising from one of the ponds.

Opposite Looking down on the garden shows how the relatively stark built structure has been transformed by luxuriant and imaginative planting. The prolific *Rosa* 'Rambling Rector' has engulfed both trellis and pergola on one side, while the climber *Rosa* 'Guinée' threatens to do the same on the other. Both roses are deliciously fragrant. The change of level and the various surface textures – reflective and matt – add greatly to the interest of the composition.

PERGOLA

Simple and sturdy, the white-painted wood will need repainting only every few years – a not impossible undertaking, as *Clematis armandii* can be cut right back in the spring, and roses can be carefully lifted away.

SHADE PLANTING

(below) Cotoneaster, camellia and *Hosta sieboldiana* 'Frances Williams' grow against the wall, pittosporum stands near the support, with containers of dwarf juniper and nicotiana.

THE STRUCTURE

This is a typical L-shaped backyard of a late nineteenth-century urban terrace house measuring 9 x 6 m/30 x 20 ft. Its principal design features are the pergola, which emphasizes the width of what is otherwise a constricted narrow space, a substantial east-facing border and two ponds that echo the rectangular lines of the garden, reflect light and – through the play of the small fountain – bring movement and sound. The choice of the creamy-white marble chippings not only adds an extra texture to the ground surfaces, but also lightens what could easily be a rather gloomy backyard. Atmospheric pollution will progressively blacken them, calling for raking and, in the longer term, periodic replacing.

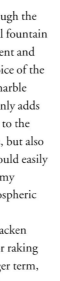

THE PATIO

The area outside the kitchen doors has been tiled to give the feeling of an outdoor room and left unplanted so that it can be easily swept clean. Jasmine, trained along the south-facing wall, adds fragrance when in bloom.

WATER FEATURES

Having two ponds not only adds extra surface interest, but is practical as waterlilies and moving water are not compatible. Simply constructed and lined with butyl rubber, the ponds are kept clean by a filter system which, like the underwater pump for the fountain, should, in the interests of safety, be installed and serviced by a qualified electrician.

THE PLANTING

This small garden is a lesson in the importance of climbers in a very restricted space, for this way an abundance of colour can be had without encroaching on the ground space. Other plants in the main border have also been chosen because they carry their flowers on spires, thus increasing the amount of colour relative to the space they take up. None of the groupings is labour intensive. The small group of perennials will need dividing every so many years and occasional staking, but little else. Attention, however, should be paid to enriching the soil, seeing that the roses are fed in season, and that the containers are kept well watered. In addition, because they are seen at such close quarters, all the plants would look better if they were kept dead-headed. Every season is catered for in this garden: the year opens with a modest flush of snowdrops, muscari and narcissi tucked into the beds and closes with the scarlet berries of the cotoneaster and the glowing sunset tints of the Virginia creeper on the pergola, leaving an evergreen backdrop of shrubs with varying leaf shapes and textures.

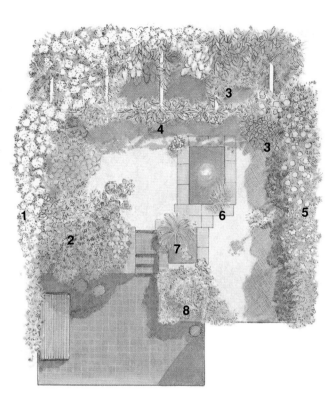

EAST BORDER

1 Along the back wall are two climbing roses, 'Rambling Rector' and 'William Lobb', *Jasminum officinale*, variegated ivy and an espaliered apricot tree.

2 Shrubs include *Viburnum tinus*, a dwarf white rhododendron, an azalea, and an escallonia; *Pieris* 'Forest Flame' contributes spring colour and *Rosa* 'Gloire de Guilan' adds further summer colour. Ground cover includes a prostrate salix, *Euonymus fortunei* and *Ajuga reptans*. Among the perennials and biennials are *Anemone hupehensis* 'September Charm', delphiniums, hollyhocks, tradescantia, euphorbia and lupins.

SOUTH WALL AND PERGOLA

3 Shade-tolerant plants include *Skimmia japonica*, camellia, cotoneaster, pittosporum, hydrangea, hosta and astilbe.

4 All the vertical surfaces support climbers and wall shrubs: evergreen *Clematis armandii* and jasmine provide year-round foliage; and Virginia creeper (*Parthenocissus quinquefolia*) adds autumn colour.

WEST WALL

5 A background planting of variegated ivy covers lower unsightly areas of wall; roses, however, are the most significant plants: 'Blush Noisette', 'Guinée' and 'Gloire de Dijon' make a mix of pretty soft colours and heady scent. They require dead-heading, careful annual pruning and periodic tying-in, demanding but rewarding tasks.

WATER PLANTING

6 As marginal plants and waterlilies do not flourish in moving water, there are only grasses in one corner of the larger pond that contains the fountain.

7 The smaller, deeper, still pond has *Iris laevigata* and waterlilies in submerged planting baskets. All need periodic lifting and dividing but no regular maintenance.

THE GREY COLLECTION

8 Next to the little pond is a collection of sun-loving grey foliage plants, many of which have fragrant leaves: santolina, lavender, *Stachys byzantina*, artemisia, *Salvia officinalis* and white *Dianthus* 'Mrs Sinkins'. These are complemented by pots of white agapanthus and white hydrangea and, in a large tub next to the house, an evergreen jasmine. As so few plants are needed, it is worth treating the dianthus as a biennial and replacing it every two years; santolina and lavender require clipping annually but the other plants only need cutting back when they outgrow their allotted space.

Below Delphinium hybrids are hardy perennials that are valuable for their vertical spires of bloom.

Right In the first garden, a formal paved central enclosure is held in by low cushions of *Hedera helix* and sections of low clipped yew hedge and is framed by flowering trees, shrubs and perennials. The pink *Hydrangea* 'Preziosa' on the right is echoed by pink *Hydrangea aspera macrophylla* on the other side. A delightful aerial hedge of pleached lime marks the entrance to, and defines, the second garden.

Left Looking back from the second garden towards the first, the eye is drawn along the full length of the vista by the brilliant red blooms in the vase and in the pots at the end. There are no other brightly coloured flowers in the garden: it is largely a tapestry of green. On the left the feathery foliage of a clump of bamboo (*Fargesia murieliae*) makes a good contrast to the glossy dark green leaves of a tree ivy (*Hedera helix*).

A TWO-ROOMED GARDEN

It is surprising how seldom a long narrow rectangular back garden is divided into sections. This brilliant little Dutch garden, designed by Dick Beyer, should inspire anyone to adopt just such a solution, for it transforms a long narrow site into two highly effective garden rooms – one symmetrical and formal, held in by clipped yew hedges and with a handsome vase as a focal point at its centre; the other asymmetrical and defined by an aerial hedge of pleached lime. By banishing grass in favour of paving and clipped ivy, and by planting shrubs and ground-cover perennials such as hardy geraniums and tiarella, a remarkably stylish easily maintained garden has been achieved. An hour or two a week at most, plus clipping, pruning, fertilizing and an annual clear-up, will keep this little garden in top form. You could create two rooms with a more distinctly different 'feel'. The aerial hedge makes only a lightweight divider: you could create a more solid one with, say, trellis, and emphasize difference by different treatment underfoot. None of this would particularly increase the maintenance.

TERRACE

A paved area close to the house has space for seating and for two wooden Versailles tubs which flank the entrance to the first garden. The terrace is south-facing, so it could include a space for culinary herbs. The tubs, like any containers, need a good deal of attention, especially watering in summer, but they do offer an opportunity for seasonal planting. However, they are not essential to the scheme, and could equally well be replaced by a pair of obelisks or finials which would require no maintenance at all.

PAVING

Except for a small square at the centre of the first garden, the paving throughout is of 30 x 30 cm/12 x 12 in slabs. This has the advantage of unifying the whole area, and slabs are the least expensive of hard surface materials, as well as one of the easiest to keep clean. However, the effect would be enriched by using stone, brick or setts (or a mixture of these), provided they were laid in such a way as to echo and emphasize the ground-level pattern.

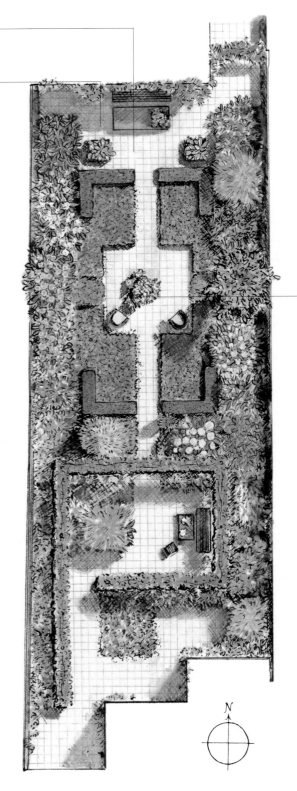

FOCAL POINT

The vase, like the Versailles tubs, brings the chance to have a splash of year-round colour in the centre of the garden. It would be simple, and not overly extravagant, to keep it stocked at other seasons with bulbs, or winter pansies, in addition to summer bedding such as petunias and gardenias. However, it could be replaced by any ornamental feature that can be viewed from all sides – a sundial, a column or obelisk. Here the vase has been used as the centrepiece of a tableau of pots, emphasized by their platform of brick which has been set into the paving.

THE STRUCTURE

The 21 x 7.25 m /73 x 23 ft rectangular space, lying between high boundary walls, is divided geometrically into what are in effect two smaller internal gardens. This is a garden of squares and rectangles. A bench under the wall of the house looks along its central axis. The first garden follows precisely the lines of the outer boundary, but its paved square centre gives it an illusion of width. Here, the formal symmetry of the design is emphasized by the crisp corners of the yew hedging, and by the neat blocks of ivy at ground level. In the second garden – a wider rectangle delineated by tall pleached limes – symmetry is replaced by geometric blocks of looser planting and a paved area leads to a garden shed.

N

THE PLANTING

This is a planting of well-tried small trees, shrubs, climbers and perennials that enhance the geometry of the design, and allow maintenance to be kept to a minimum. Annual work will include limited staking of perennials, dead-heading in summer, some pruning of shrubs, clipping the yew hedge and ivy, and pleaching the limes. The perennials would need lifting and dividing every five years or so, but this could be staggered. Like any other town garden, this needs an annual dressing of fertilizer, and the addition every few years of a layer of good compost.

FIRST GARDEN

1 The tubs are planted with *Hosta sieboldiana* 'Frances Williams'.
2 Four segments of yew hedging (*Taxus baccata*) frame the internal rectangle.
3 An evergreen ground-covering of ivy forms blocks that outline the central square.
4 and 5 The cross axes are block planted with *Tiarella cordifolia* and *Alchemilla mollis*.
6 A substantial *Viburnum plicatum* 'Mariesii', and two small trees, *Prunus* x *subhirtella* 'Autumnalis' and *Cornus kousa* are underplanted with hostas

and *Cimicifuga simplex*.
7 *Prunus* 'Trailblazer' stands in the middle.
8 *Rosa* 'New Dawn' and clematis clothe the wall.
9 *Hydrangea serrata* 'Blue Bird' and *H. aspera macrophylla*.
10 Beside the terrace, *Geranium macrorrhizum* 'Spessart' surrounds *Viburnum* x *bodnantense* 'Dawn'.
11 *Hydrangea* 'Preciosa' grows behind the yew hedge.
12 The wall is clothed with *Hydrangea anomala petiolaris*.
13 *Rhododendron hunnewellianum* 'Cunningham's White' backs this section of yew hedge.
14 In the section between the two gardens *Pyrus salicifolia* 'Pendula' is planted behind

Below Tiarella cordifolia, an evergreen shade-tolerant ground cover, has frothy white flowers in late spring.

Gypsophila 'Rosenschleier'.
15 *Viburnum* x *bodnantense* 'Dawn' and *Parrotia persica* are underplanted with *Anemone* x *hybrida* 'Königin Charlotte', *Geranium macrorrhizum* 'Spessart' and *Campanula lactiflora* 'Prichard's Variety'.

SECOND GARDEN

16 An aerial hedge of pleached limes (*Tilia cordata*) delineates the space.
17 *Fargesia murieliae* dominates the larger block in the north-west corner, which also contains *Gypsophila* 'Rosenschleier', *Echinacea purpurea*, *Anemone* x *hybrida* 'Honorine Jobert', *Campanula lactiflora*, *Eupatorium purpureum*,

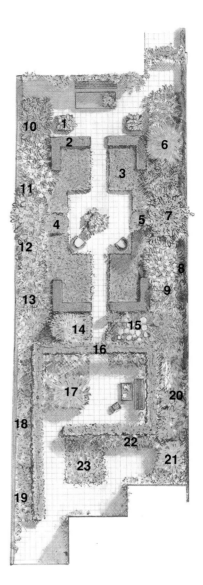

Helleborus foetidus, *Geranium endressii* and *Hosta sieboldiana elegans*.
18 *Rosa* 'Lykkefund' grows against the wall.
19 The narrow shady border contains *Tiarella cordifolia*, *Decaisnea fargesii*, *Alchemilla mollis* and *Helleborus foetidus*.
20 In the east border

behind the pleached limes are *Cimicifuga simplex*, *Rodgersia aesculifolia* and *Viburnum plicatum* 'Mariesii'.
21 *Aucuba japonica* dominates the corner.
22 *Viburnum tinus* is planted with arborescent *Hedera helix* and *Hosta sieboldiana elegans*.
23 *Brunnera macrophylla*.

Right The pleasing geometry of the garden can be particularly well appreciated when it is seen from an upper storey room.

Left The planting of the central parterre is of the simplest kind; its spokes are infilled with clipped *Santolina pinnata neapolitana*, the sundial and edges softened with creeping ivy. You could raise the height of the centre piece or reduce the size of the hedge around it to reveal more of the pedestal.

A SECLUDED TOWN GARDEN

This ingenious formal garden, designed by Christopher Masson, is full of illusions. Although it is an ordinary rectangular town garden, its boundaries have been obscured by the planting so that attention is drawn instead to the curves of beds within this frame; two pairs of what appear to be stately gate piers leading who knows where further accentuate the garden's width; and although there is no lawn, the overall effect is cool and green. This dignified formality is, however, broken by the planting which has been deliberately made to erupt out over the boundaries of the containing beds.

The triumph is the achievement of a grand effect with only modest materials: gravel, old brick and trellis. The brick piers are of extremely simple construction, as is the trellis that frames the garden. Together they give the design powerful vertical architectural accents which also ensure privacy and act as supports for climbers.

The display of container plants is dispensable and apart from the clipping of the box and santolina and some tidying of the climbers, the labour input largely depends upon the planting within the borders. The present owners usually spend a couple of hours a week in the garden during the growing season and make time for one or two annual blitzes.

THE STRUCTURE

The garden measures about 10.5 x 6.5 m/45 x 25 ft overall. In such a small space it was a bold decision to confine the cultivated area to the furthest two thirds of the garden, freeing a broad swathe next to the house for use as an open-air room that is dotted with containers and with a table and chairs for alfresco meals. It is essentially an inward-looking garden conceived to secure privacy. One of the design's principal objects is to emphasize the garden's width: it does this by means of the flanking brick piers – which suggest that avenues or pergolas lead off to right and left of the garden – and the curving shapes of the parterre and north border. The absence of high-maintenance grass in favour of easy-care gravel is compensated for by an evergreen box parterre and the abundant evergreen shrubbery which forms the garden's backcloth.

BRICKWORK

The choice of old brick, which complements the house, is used as the linking hard-surface element: it edges the beds, makes the short path to the seat, and forms the piers. The piers are an unusual but arresting feature; the contrast between the taller flanking ones and the shorter ones either side of the seat provides an intriguing and false perspective.

FOCAL POINT

The hub of the composition is a sphere sundial but care must be taken that its contours are not engulfed by ivy. An urn or finial of not less than 1.5 m/5 ft high would be equally striking.

THE GRAVEL

The pale-coloured small pea gravel brings light into the garden and is the most comfortable to walk on. It should be laid over a good base with a built-in drainage system. In cities, atmospheric pollution will gradually blacken it, calling for periodic raking. Weeds are easily coped with by an annual application of herbicide.

THE PLANTING

The survival of plants in this garden is radically affected by the extremely poor soil; by the stagnant bowl of air in which, like so many other town gardens, it is caught; and by a large lime tree and plane tree, which suck in moisture and give fairly dense shade during the summer months. This means that despite regular soil and foliar feeding, some plants will not survive and each year some gaps need to be filled. The nature of the planting changes as it moves from the deep shade of the border into sunlight at the back of the house, a progression from common laurel and hostas to roses and wisteria. The massed shrubbery of evergreens and the climbers and wall shrubs that clothe the two side walls screen out whatever lies beyond the garden. Without the containers which offer additional bloom but are not essential to the garden's success, the workload would be minimal: fertilizing, general tidying up, and some weeding and cutting back, together with annual pruning, tying-in and some plant replacement. The potential workload has been substantially reduced by introducing a computerized surface watering system.

BORDER SCREENING
1 Shade-tolerant evergreens form the background: *Fargesia murieliae, Prunus laurocerasus, Ligustrum ovalifolium* and *Pittosporum tobira.*
2 Behind the seat is *Ilex aquifolium* 'Golden Milkboy'.
3 In the centre is a mixed planting of *Mahonia japonica, Hydrangea macrophylla, Nandina domestica,* a standard *Rosa* 'Iceberg' and *Olearia* x *macrodonta.*
4 The foreground planting includes *Euphorbia characias wulfenii,* pulmonaria, *Iris sibirica,* Japanese Anemone, peonies, *Phormium tenax* and *Hosta fortunei obscura.*
5 The border is contained by a clipped box hedge.
6 *Hebe subalpina, Polygonatum odoratum* and *Yucca filamentosa* grow through the gravel.

FLANKING PIERS
7 These support *Rosa* 'Félicité Perpétue', white *R.* 'Iceberg', *R.* 'Phyllis Bide', *Clematis campaniflora* and *Hedera helix* 'Goldheart'.

SOUTH BORDER
8 *Betula pendula, Choisya ternata* 'Sundance' and a fig tree are underplanted with tellima, bergenia, *Cotoneaster horizontalis* and *Hosta* 'Frances Williams'.

NORTH BORDER
9 White *Rosa bracteata,* a standard *Lonicera periclymenum* 'Belgica', *Myrtus communis tarentina, Convolvulus cneorum, Ceanothus* 'Cascade', *Buddleja* 'Lochinch' and *Clematis*

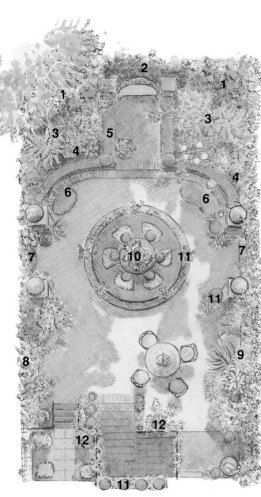

'Comtesse de Bouchaud' are underplanted with *Phlomis fruticosa, Artemisia* 'Powis Castle', pink lavender, *Geranium endressii, Ruta graveolens, Alchemilla mollis, Caryopteris* x *clandonensis, Hosta sieboldiana elegans* and violas.

PARTERRE
10 The parterre is of dwarf box infilled with *Santolina pinnata neapolitana.* Ivy is entwined round the sundial.

CONTAINER ACCENTS
11 Clipped box adds formal accents, while perlargoniums bring colour to the central parterre.
12 Next to the house there is an impressive array of container-grown plants including agapanthus, *Solanum jasminoides, Pittosporum tobira, Trachelospermum asiaticum, Olea europaea* and *Argyranthemum frutescens.*

Below Bergenia cordifolia, an evergreen perennial that tolerates sun or shade and is frost-hardy.

A CHECKER-BOARD YARD

It is no mean achievement to find a successful solution to one of the most depressing of garden sites – a small urban backyard. Here the Dutch designer Mien Ruys has managed to make an unusual yet highly satisfying composition out of a space hemmed in by buildings. It draws on elements of the time-honoured Dutch formal garden tradition, but re-casts them in an intriguing abstract pattern that is particularly striking when viewed from above. Carefully avoiding all vistas and focal points, the designer has created a garden devised to be moved around in and looked at from several sides – as the disposition of the chairs indicates.

Taking the cue from the paving slabs, the garden is divided into three areas whose shapes are square or rectangular. Nearest the house is an open terrace. Next follows a pair of bold rectangular beds, subdivided into smaller rectangles and filled with perennials and blocks of low-clipped box. Furthest away a series of small beds filled with roses and culinary herbs, some edged with box, occupies a rectangular area. Straight narrow beds along the perimeter occasionally widen into rectangles that serve to delineate each of the three areas. Pleached and mophead trees and climbers along the perimeters add essential verticals as well as provide aerial screening.

The large proportion of paving and restricted but choice planting makes this a very easy garden to maintain. Extensive use has been made of box not only to edge beds, but as square cushions which, in effect, take the place of grass, and of ground-cover plants which, once established, will smother weeds and require little attention.

With its interesting contrasts of leaf shapes and textures, and its highlights of whites and creams scattered across a grey and green canvas, this garden exudes an atmosphere of quiet contemplation.

Right The view from an upstairs window shows the architectural structure of this tiny back garden. The squares of low, clipped box fulfil the soothing, evergreen role usually played by grass. The foreground beds, in the shape of blocks echoing the box squares and paving, are filled with a predominantly green and white planting of pulmonaria, gypsophila, alchemilla, hostas, phlox and delphiniums. A screen of pollarded acacias and tall shrubs on the left and climbing roses on the right helps to provide privacy.

Above Looking back towards the house, the tiny beds of herbs are seen just beyond an arching *Rosa* 'Iceberg'. On the left, the beds are filled with bolder groups of *Senecio* "Sunshine', *Acanthus mollis* and *Bergenia* 'Silberlicht'.

THE STRUCTURE

The garden which measures 12 x 5 m/42 x 16 ft runs south-north from the back of the house. Its simple grid pattern could be easily adapted to suit other small town gardens. The easiest approach would be to draw up a scheme on graph paper. If you want to include herbs, locate them where they would get the most sun. The evergreen element – here dwarf box – is essential to the design's success; it provides strong geometry even in winter.

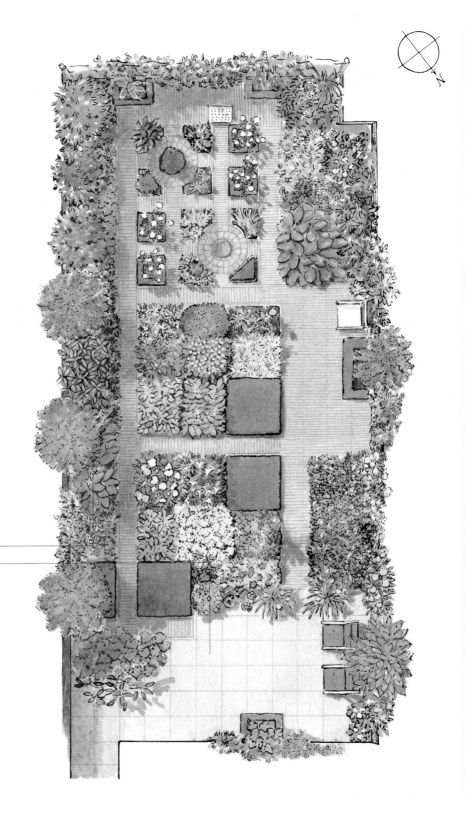

CROSS AXIS (*above*)
Looking east-west across the centre of the garden, standard feathery mophead acacias, interspersed with shrubs, form an aerial screen in front of adjacent houses. The pools of restful green of the clipped box contrast with the pale feathery foliage and flowers.

PAVING
Narrow grey bricks echo the colour of the concrete paving slabs that make up the terrace. They align with the garden's rectangular shapes, making a very subdued ground-level pattern. An intriguing exception has been made in the herb garden where two circles of setts surround a birdbath and a box cone.

THE PLANTING

Instead of a confused and restless mass of spot planting, there has been a disciplined choice of perennials planted in sizeable blocks. The use of whites, pale pinks and creams adds light to the scheme – an important point in a town garden where light is at a premium. Much of the

Above Rosa 'Graham Thomas', a repeat flowering new English climbing rose with a strong tea rose fragrance.

planting consists of perennials, which need little maintenance other than to be lifted and divided every three or so years, and shrubs that need annual pruning or clipping: the limes could be replaced with climbers that are easier to maintain. The beds do need regular grooming, but in such a minute space the work should not be onerous.

1 Most of the evergreen element is dwarf box (*Buxus sempervirens* 'Suffruticosa').

PERIMETER BEDS
2 Limes (*Tilia platyphyllos*) arising from box-edged beds are being pleached to make an aerial screen. Two tall posts support lateral wires onto which the young branches are tied. They will require hard pruning every winter. A rose climbs between them.
3 Shrubs including *Viburnum* x *bodnantense* are underplanted with *Sedum telephium*, Japanese anemones, *Tanacetum vulgare* and *Lysimachia ephemerum*.
4 The central section of the bed is dominated by three mophead acacias (*Robinia pseudoacacia* 'Umbraculifera').
5 *Viburnum rhytidophyllum* is underplanted with *Lysimachia clethroides*.
6 Variegated holly is underplanted with nicotiana and *Hosta sieboldiana elegans* and a cushion of box.
7 *Acanthus spinosus*, *Bergenia* 'Silberlicht', *Euphorbia characias*; *Gaura lindheimeri* and *Senecio* 'Sunshine' fill the corner bed.
8 *Rosa* 'Blanche Double de Coubert'.
9 *Rosa* 'Graham Thomas'.
10 A sorbus is planted in a box-edged bed.
11 *Rosa* 'Seagull' clambers over an arch.
12 *Rosa* 'Easlea's Golden Rambler' grows above ground-covering *Waldsteina ternata* and arborescent ivy.
13 *Catalpa bignonioides*.
14 Pots of *Hydrangea macrophylla* 'Madame Emile Mouillère'.
15 A box-edged bed contains *Macleaya cordata* and *Clematis montana rubens* .
16 Pots of *Hydrangea aspera*.
17 Pots of agapanthus and *Spiraea japonica*.

NEAR BED
18 Two cushions of box are supplemented by *Pulmonaria officinalis* 'Sissinghurst White', gypsophila, *Alchemilla mollis*, *Phlox paniculata*, *Helleborus orientalis*, *Lilium regale* and *Platycodon grandiflorus* 'Perlmutterschale'.

CENTRAL BED
19 A single cushion of box is balanced by *Hosta fortunei albopicta*, *Astrantia major*, *Delphinium* 'Völkerfrieden', *Anaphalis margaritacea*, *Achillea ptarmica* 'The Pearl', *Verbascum nigrum*, *Helleborus* x *sternii* and *Stachys byzantina*.

HERB GARDEN
20 Four box-edged beds contain roses: 'Iceberg', 'Blanche Double de Coubert', 'Apricot Nectar' and 'Nevada'. The eight tiny spandrel beds have culinary herbs in season.

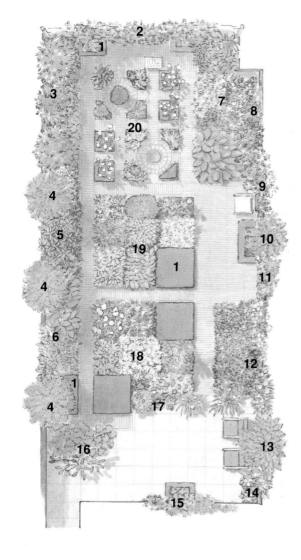

Left A view over the entrance pergola, festooned in wisteria and *Rosa* 'Zéphirine Drouhin', shows the garden's firm ground plan: a split-level octagon lawn held in by paths and encompassing borders and pergolas.

Right Two formal rectangular beds edged with box flank the terrace; each contains a standard *Viburnum carlesii* underplanted with *Rosa* 'The Fairy'.

A FORMAL LAWN GARDEN

The uniquely pleasurable tactile quality of evenly clipped grass has long been rated highly among a garden's delights – indeed, the idea of a garden without a lawn as its centrepiece is unthinkable for many people. Soft and inviting, here it contrasts with the garden's hard landscape and also provides children with a safe area on which to play.

Arabella Lennox-Boyd's design enshrines the lawn at the heart of this garden. The interest generated by its bold octagonal lines, emphasized by brick borders, is further increased by setting it on two levels: one steps down into the central sunken area as into a shallow pool, or as onto a dance floor. Its shape dictates those of the encompassing beds and, beneath a mature horse chestnut tree, a pleasant terrace for sitting.

Two pergolas add height to the composition. One acts as a frontispiece to the garden, the other ensures privacy; both provide welcome shade in summer and straddle gravel paths. There is a succession of flower interest through the seasons. Spring brings flowering camellias, clematis, azalea, vibur-nums, mahonias, the flowering cherry and the horse chestnut. Summer follows with peonies, clematis and roses. In the autumn the leaves of the prunus contribute bright orange and red.

Two hours work a week in season should keep this garden in perfect condition. It is clearly important that the lawn is well tended, and mowed regularly in the growing season, a process made easier by the brick surrounds. But since it is so small an area, its upkeep is unlikely to be onerous. There is obviously some weeding, clipping, pruning and tying-in to do in the planting surrounding the lawn, and no town garden can go unenriched in terms of soil additives but a composition such as this, in which fairly relaxed planting is firmly held in by built formal structure, is not demanding – provided there has been no skimping in the early stages of its planning and construction.

Container plants need regular watering but they are not an essential ingredient of this scheme. Come the autumn, the mighty horse chestnut will shed its leaves and these will need to be cleared.

THE STRUCTURE

Two narrow gardens were combined to make a single area of about 8 m/ 24 ft square behind tall terraced houses. A pergola runs the whole length of the north-west side of the garden, sited to secure privacy and access to a back gate. A second, shorter, pergola along the southern side spans the entrance to the garden which is approached across a bridge over a basement area. The remaining space has been formalized by insetting an octagon of lawn at the centre enclosed by narrow brick paths. This creates four spandrels; one is a terrace which, facing south-west, enjoys the afternoon sun and a fine view of the pergolas. The other three are planted as mixed borders. The main features of this strong design could be rearranged to suit a different site. The long pergola could either abut the house, for example, or be placed opposite it. The approach to the garden could equally be from the south or east side, dispensing with the box-edged beds. For a narrower site the western pergola arcade could be dropped, keeping only its projecting arch.

PERGOLAS (*left*)
These add an extra storey of colour and interest to the garden as well as providing seclusion and shade. The entrances from the pergolas to the lawn are accentuated by brick paths lined with clipped dwarf box. The view back into the long pergola terminates with a large terracotta pot, planted with a variegated evergreen shrub. Good design and sound structure are essential for pergolas: they are in focus year-round, and must stand alone in the winter months as worthwhile garden architecture. They should never be less than 2.2 m/8 ft high or 2 m/6 ft wide, for plants soon encroach on the space inside. They may be made from wood, as here, which, however well treated with preservatives, will call for maintenance and, eventually, replacement. Other options include brick or reconstituted stone pillars; or iron or plasticized alloy elements. A wide range of ready-made pergolas is available; choose one that complements the style of your house, and one that is robust enough to support the weight of the climbers.

LAWNS

The lawn at the heart of this garden draws the eye at every point. It must, therefore, be of the finest turf and maintained to an impeccable level. It calls for regular attention – for mowing, watering, feeding and weeding – but as the area is so small, the task need not be daunting. An alternative to the grass would be to widen the surrounding paths and make the inner octagon a pond. This would reflect light into the garden and offer opportunities for displays of waterlilies and marginal plants. For less maintenance, either the central lawn or the marginal lawns could be paved. But in this case the paving itself should become a decorative feature, laid in an interesting pattern, perhaps using contrasting materials and allowing spaces for ground-hugging plants to take root and sprawl. If the inner octagon was paved, an urn or sundial would provide an attractive vertical focal point.

THE PLANTING

Apart from the grass, much of the planting is of shade-tolerant plants, as this is essentially a shadowy garden enclosed partly by large, mature trees and partly by the pergolas. Massed evergreen shrubs set off the relatively few flowers which form the foreground of the borders, and the colour comes chiefly from the climbers on both pergolas. Most of the regular input is in keeping the grass in perfect condition, and watering the containers, but the climbers need keeping under control, the borders benefit from attention and clipped evergreens need the occasional manicure as well as annual attention. The climbers and shrubs will, of course, require more serious work at the appropriate pruning season, and the soil needs enriching annually.

LONG PERGOLA
1 This supports *Rosa* 'New Dawn', *Clematis montana*, *C*. 'Perle d'Azur' and *C*. 'Marie Boisselot'.
2 The wall is covered with ivy.
3 The gravel path is lined with silver-margined *Euonymus fortunei* 'Silver Queen'.

SHORT PERGOLA
4 This supports *Rosa* 'Zéphirine Drouhin', *Lonicera periclymenum* and *Wisteria sinensis*.

Below Prunus 'Amanogawa' is a spring-flowering fastigiate tree with good autumn foliage.

BOX-EDGED BEDS
5 Beneath standard *Viburnum carlesii*, the ground is planted with *Rosa* 'The Fairy', which comes into flower after the spring bulbs and forget-me-nots are over.

NORTH BORDER
6 Shaded by the pergola and a large lime tree in a neighbouring garden, this bed is planted with *Mahonia media, Viburnum davidii*, camellia, azalea, *Halesia tetraptera* (syn *H. carolina*), euphorbias, astilbe, bergenia and ferns of all sorts including *Osmunda regalis*.

WEST BORDER
7 In front of the larger evergreen shrubs that include camellia, there are hostas, hellebores, grey-leaved artemesias and hebes, and *Iris sibirica*.

SOUTH BORDER
8 This is dominated by a flowering tree, *Prunus* 'Amanogawa'.
9 Beneath the evergreen shrubs, including *Viburnum davidii*, are silver-leaved artemisias and hebes. White roses and a tree peony add further seasonal interest.

CONTAINERS
10 Clipped box balls accentuate the way in and out of both pergolas; and a few other containers of tender flowering plants bring touches of seasonal colour to the terrace.

GARDENS
for the
TIME-WATCHER

Previous pages This beautifully controlled garden is a careful balance of high- and low-maintenance areas. The design is made up of a series of asymmetrical rectangles of brick paving, lawn and beds. Most of the latter are shrub-filled, but there is one glorious complex border of flowers calling for tending all through the season: that is clearly the garden's showpiece. Hedges have been kept to an accessible height for easy trimming.

The seven gardens which follow are achieved on a weekly input during the growing season of about an afternoon a week. Like the gardens in the previous chapter, they also need extra attention in the spring and autumn when more serious prolonged work is needed to cut down, lift and divide perennials, prune and train shrubs, move and replace any unsatisfactory plants and fertilize. What principally sets these gardens apart from those discussed earlier is the elaboration in the planting. With these gardens we enter the world of more serious plantsmanship; but it is of a kind which can be quantified in terms of time. What anyone who has limited time wishes to avoid is everything having to be done at once. This, with careful planning, can easily be achieved. All that it calls for as you elaborate your planting is to select plants that stagger their calls on your attention through the year. This means, for example, selecting shrubs which will need pruning after flowering in addition to those which require it during the winter months or spring.

With more and more unusual plants the possible garden effects multiply. The herb garden becomes a possibility. Herbs need careful nurture. They tend to sprawl and become untidy, demanding a wary eye, annual cutting down and frequent replanting. A clear geometric framework helps to discipline these attractive but unruly plants. Mixed shrub and herbaceous borders will be another opportunity. These must be carefully planned for a succession of bloom and many of the plants will need staking and cutting back during the season. The beds will also need weeding. A full range of herbaceous plants is there to be selected from. The classic components of borders are the perennials like asters, heleniums, helianthus and penstemons, all of which will need periodic division and staking. You can also include biennials, like aquilegia, foxgloves and hollyhocks, which will self-seed once established. Many gardeners add extra colour to borders by filling gaps with annuals; some of these are self-seeders such as poppies and nigella, others will be bought-in bedding plants; both will add another dimension to the garden picture.

The potential of garden forms like the parterre increases: instead of setting clipped box shapes against coloured gravels, use them to outline beds filled with flowers. These could consist of medium-maintenance perennials intermixed with bulbs for a spring display, or seasonal bedding plants that you buy in and plant out each season.

In a small space some of the biggest opportunities come with

Left A lesson in good garden design in a very confined space boldly uses hard surface elements – treillage, an urn, and piers topped with pineapple finials – matched by equally positive plant interest. Vertical accents exploit foliage contrasts, both sculpted and free-ranging – fine-textured box topiary, ivy trained up the piers, and the looser habit of the golden hop. The freer forms of the helichrysum sprays and the smooth, pleated leaves of *Hosta sieboldiana* make contrasting focal points.

Dividing a long rectangular space into two contrasting areas can double the interest of your garden. Both of these restful, predominantly green gardens are relatively easy to maintain. The first is a box parterre in gravel with ground-cover planting of glossy-leaved vinca held in by an aerial wall of pleached limes. Once established the limes call only for annual clipping and pruning. The box hedges are quick to cut, but trimming the domes and spirals would be more time-consuming. A spring planting of tulips would be lovely in the beds and would take little time to achieve. A second garden beyond has a manicured lawn surrounded by beds planted with lavender and a low containing hedge of yew.

climbers such as roses, clematis, vines, abutilon and wisteria, for they can almost double the plant and flower capacity. Climbers can be trained up the wall of the house, along fences, through trellis, over summerhouses and arbours, through trees and shrubs and up and over arches and pergolas. But they will often call for dead-heading, pruning and careful tying-in. Choose them according to their colour and habit and flowering season.

Water features beyond the simplest small pond or wall fountain can also be yours. These embrace the more complex movement of water by means of an electric pump producing fountains and cascades. Remember that anything to do with water in this sense is potentially dangerous and is best installed by a professional for reasons of safety. Water also means that the world of aquatic plants is open to exploration, with pretty effects to be obtained through combinations of waterlilies and marginals.

More complex training effects can be essayed either in free-standing formal shapes to punctuate the design or as linear patterns to form screens and hedges. The process takes time, but as plants mature they will assume the status of horticultural art. Topiary, the art of training yew or box plants into shape, adds distinction to any garden, architectural or otherwise. Ready-trained topiary is available but expensive. It is not, however, a complicated art to master, although unless you have a sure eye, it is best to stick at first to simple geometric shapes of ball, cube, cone or obelisk. It is also possible to buy ready-formed wire frames in a greater variety of shapes, including birds and beasts, which simply require you to wait until they fill out before you go to work with your shears.

With a greater input of time, training effects, particularly with trees, can be multiplied. Instead of two mopheads, for instance, six or eight will make a modest stately avenue; instead of a single specimen

This tiny plant lover's town garden is beautifully paved with small brick that swept clean makes a perfect foil for plant forms. Slight variations in level, a modest water feature and a simple arbour add structural interest. All of the owner's energy is devoted to maintaining a balanced mixture of climbers, small evergreen and flowering shrubs and ground-cover perennials such as hardy geraniums. The restricted palette of flower colour tones with the pinky-red brick.

Left Structure plays a crucial role in achieving an illusion of garden order at all times of the year. Even without the labour-intensive containers, this composition of a central path, emphasized by clipped box, leading to a small, raised terrace with a wooden pergola atop four reconstituted stone columns would be strikingly successful.

Right Immaculately kept focal points deflect the vision from untidiness. Here the pretty neo-classical pavilion with its neatly clipped domes of box fills the eye, turning the autumnal muddle around it into an irrelevance in what is a satisfying garden picture. Lawns with deciduous trees anywhere near them risk becoming patterned with leaves. Enjoy the sight as an ephemeral pleasure – then sweep up! The stone edging to the lawn is labour-saving if it is sited out of the way of the mower's blade. The flanking shrub borders need little regular attention but will soon be due for the annual blitz of pruning and tidying.

tree, to take another example, a tunnel of laburnum becomes a possibility. Free-standing fruit trees can be trained as domes or goblets; and fruit trees in espalier, cordon or fan shapes can be grown against a wall or tied into a framework of wires or fencing to make a garden division or screen. For a small space, always select a fruit tree on a dwarf rooting stock.

Containers can be considered. They are, of course, demanding, for they call for soil change, feeding and watering; and the smaller they are, the more work they entail. Joy, however, resides in the fact that the possibilities for their ever-changing contents and positions means

Choosing a colour theme provides beds of mixed medium-maintenance planting with an instant identity. The keynote for the bed is set by the year-round curtain of 'Goldheart' ivy on the wall. The gold variegation of the ivy is echoed in the *Hosta fortunei aureomarginata* and the yellow-green foliage of *Filipendula ulmaria* 'Aurea' at ground level. The flowers – *Anemone* x *hybrida* 'Honorine Jobert', *Agapanthus campanulatus albidus*, *Clematis* 'Alba Luxurians', *Lysimachia clethroides* – are predominantly white, with a shadowing of mauve from *Viola cornuta*. The centrepiece is spiky *Astelia chathamica* in a terracotta vase.

endless permutations of their use. Vases and troughs as part of the garden scene provide opportunities for a sequence of planting through the year from spring bulbs to summer bedding and winter pansies. Used singly or in groups they can form focal points, or can be used to emphasize the ground-level geometry of a garden – along a path or around an ornament. Large, immovable ones, like classical vases, can hold the whole composition of a small garden together, and have the added advantage of being able to be filled with a variety of colour. Containers are also exciting because they are available in so many shapes – from historical to contemporary, and materials – stone,

reconstituted stone, iron, ceramic, terracotta, wood and fibreglass (which, as it is so lightweight, is useful if it needs to be moved).

In this middle range of commitment, balance should be the aim. Decide which of the more elaborate horticultural elements you would most like. (I would start with only one or two. If you become addicted you can easily multiply them.) Let these be the focus of your energies and offset their demands by organizing the rest of the garden on structural low-maintenance lines. Always remember to keep the structural parts in tip-top shape, for they are the essential foil that holds the remainder in good order.

Purple-red tones characterize the planting and act as a foil to the striking green leaf shapes – spiky iris, palmate abutilon, serrated *Melianthus major*. The tapestry of plants in the background – *Cytisus battandieri*, *Clematis viticella* 'Purpurea Plena Elegans' and *Jasminum officinale* 'Argenteovariegatum' – combines with purple-leaved berberis, *Eupatorium purpureum* and the bronzy foliage of *Weigela florida* 'Foliis Purpureis' to cast murky shadows and disguise the fact that this is a narrow bed against a tall boundary wall or fence. *Phlox paniculata* 'Norah Leigh' gleams in the foreground.

A SHADY GOTHIC GARDEN

This is a brilliant and loving solution to one of the most depressing of all garden sites – a small, narrow, shady north-facing town garden. It is achieved by exploiting the shade and giving the garden a strong, identifiable style. This is immediately established by the half-hidden gothic arches leading into mysterious shadows, and reinforced by the feeling of enclosure and the long, lush grass. A galaxy of shade-loving and shade-tolerant plants is offset by climbers which reach for sunlight, while flowers in white and pastel colours, in beds and pots, scatter an illusion of light into the darkest corners. The busy owner is a committed gardener, who tries to find a little time to work in the garden most days during the growing season; but apart from the demands made by the lawn, a garden of rare and dappled mystery could be maintained by spending an afternoon each week on it.

Right The view down the length of the garden, where painted wooden gothic arches frame the entrance to a fernery. Pots of plants, including a clematis supported by a cane wigwam, are dotted along the length of the meandering path. The small area of luxuriant grass must be re-seeded annually with pre-germinated seed.

Left Looking back towards the house, a tiny secluded terrace is approached through a tangle of roses ('Russelliana', 'Souvenir de la Malmaison', 'New Dawn' and 'Buff Beauty'). The borders are crammed with shade-loving plants, among them Japanese anemones, astilbes, astrantias, euphorbias, cranesbill geraniums, hellebores, heuchera and many more.

LAWN INSETS

5 Tiny brick-edged beds include feverfew, oxalis, *Tiarella cordifolia*, wild strawberries and violets.

LAWN

6 To maintain a lawn where light hardly penetrates, this is re-sown annually with pre-germinated seed. Because of the inset beds, it is cut by hand. The result is delightful but labour-intensive.

PATHSIDE CONTAINERS

7 These include herbs as well as ornamentals. *Clematis florida* 'Flore Pleno' and *C.f.* 'Sieboldii' are trained up cane wigwams.

EAST BORDER

8 *Clematis* 'Duchess of Edinburgh', *Rosa* 'New Dawn' and *Hydrangea anomala petiolaris* clothe the wall. The lower storey includes *Dicentra spectabilis alba* and *D.* 'Pearl Drops', toad lilies, geraniums and hostas. 9 *Prunus* x *subhirtella* 'Autumnalis' dominates the east border. Camellias are planted on either side.

NARROW EAST BED

10 The wall is wreathed in *Clematis armandii*, *C.* 'Alba Luxurians', *C.* 'Duchess of Edinburgh' and *C. montana rubens*. *Hydrangea arborescens*

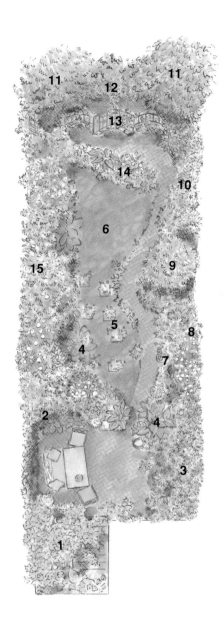

Above Spring-flowering *Clematis montana rubens* only needs pruning to restrict its vigorous growth.

'Annabelle' is underplanted with *Hosta fortunei hyacinthina*, hardy geraniums and *Campanula takesimana*. 11 *Philadelphus* 'Belle Etoile'.

FERNERY

12 This makes a virtue out of the drawbacks of

shade and recalls the Victorian fashion for ferns. They include *Adiantum pedatum*; *Asplenium scolopendrium*; *Athyrium filix-femina* forms and *A. niponicum pictum* ; *Onoclea sensibilis* ; *Osmunda regalis* ; decorative forms of *Polystichum setiferum* ;

Dryopteris dilatata, *D. filix-mas* and several forms of *D. affinis*. Ferns can be left in clumps for years and are also easily divided. The fern fronds must be cut back to the ground in spring to allow new fronds to unfurl.

GOTHIC ARCHES

13 Each side arch shelters a pyramid-shaped box in a Georgian vase, surrounded in summer with trailing lobelia. Overhead grow *Passiflora caerulea* and climbing *Rosa* 'Blairii No. 2', *R.* 'Céline Forestier', *R.* 'Félicité Perpétue' and *R.* 'New Dawn'.

LAWN BED

14 *Zantedeschia aethiopica* 'White Sails' stands out in a low-level planting of alchemilla, anaphalis, campanula, fuchsias, geraniums, white nicotiana and lime-green *N. langsdorffii*.

WEST BORDER

15 Shrubs include *Viburnum opulus* and *Hydrangea arborescens* 'Annabelle', with *Clematis armandii*, *Rosa* 'Cécile Brunner' and *R.* 'New Dawn' on the wall. In front are hostas, dicentras, foxgloves, geraniums, nicotiana, penstemons and others.

Left The main vista from the house to the gazebo. Clipped junipers act as sentinels and provide a contrast to the more informal and horizontal planting in the four spandrel beds. Notice the pleasing point counterpoint: taut path, pond and junipers; the sprawling content of the beds; the sharp lines of the hedge; and beyond that, the tapestry of trees.

Right Even under snow the formal elements will ensure a pleasing garden picture. Here the winters are so severe that standard roses are protected against frost damage.

A CLASSIC FLOWER GARDEN

Few garden plans are wholly foolproof, but this is one that is: a quartered square with a circle inscribed at the centre. This classic formula has been repeated times without number since it was first used in renaissance Italy, but no amount of repetition can erode the serenity of the composition, with its sense of balance and harmony. Here it has been adapted to a rectangular site on Long Island by the designer Adele Mitchell. She added a substantial rectangular bay with a gazebo at the far end of the garden, thus emphasizing the main vista.

The garden is contained by a low hedge of yew; this delineates the enclosing geometry, holds the encroaching woodland at bay, and provides a rich dark background against which flowers exhibit themselves to perfection. Six junipers, clipped into tall sugar loaves, provide vertical accents, and at the heart of the garden a small round pond with a jet of water brings light and animation to the garden.

Surprisingly, this garden calls for only about two hours of work a week in the growing season – weeding, dead-heading, cutting back and limited staking. The secrets of its low demand are that plants – shrubs, perennials and bulbs – are placed very close together, leaving little space for weeds, and there is also a built-in sprinkler system. Twice a year the owners have a major blitz.

This is a garden for flower-lovers. Skilfully planted, it gives a succession of colour-controlled bloom through spring, summer and autumn, while its firm bones, both built and evergreen, ensure a striking winter picture. The result is breathtaking.

THE STRUCTURE

The space measuring about 10.8 x 15 m/36 x 40 ft has been made into a square with a rectangular bay at the end (a curved exedra would be another possibility), and the designer has used one of the most enduring and satisfying of garden formulae: a square divided into four, with a circle at the centre. She has used brick paths to delineate the geometry of the garden, and the clear-cut lines of clipped hedges to enclose it. Notice the way that even in a strictly symmetrical garden, irregularities can be allowed for. Here, an immovably sited exit on the south side has been accommodated by simply bending the path round at the last minute.

CENTRAL POND

This is a simple shallow circle of water with a few lilies, some fish, and a central jet that requires an electric pump. The water adds light and movement to the garden, but a sundial, a large urn, a well-head or even a large topiary piece would also suffice to hold the composition together.

PATHS

The small size of the old bricks used in the paths makes the mixed borders seem even larger than they are. The bricks have been laid end-on to emphasize rather than conceal the length of the path from the entrance to the gazebo, but herringbone or basket-weave pattern would also be successful, and a mixture of stone, brick and small slabs would also be attractive. Whatever materials are used, the paths need careful detailing because the eye is constantly drawn to them.

GAZEBO

This is built on a handsome scale, and of antique lattice panels and wooden supports, though the back and roof are new. It is a simple enough structure and any variant of this one, including many ready-made arbours, would be suitable, provided the boldness of scale is preserved. The gazebo here is painted an eye-catching white, which stands out well against the surrounding greens, but needs to be kept in pristine condition. Off-white, greys and grey-greens would provide less startling contrast, and require less attention.

TOPIARY VERTICALS

The verticals provided by the juniper topiary are important in the garden, but other fastigiate clipped evergreens could be used: yew, box, other varieties of juniper, or fast-growing evergreens such as *Cupressus macrocarpa* or *Ilex vomitoria*. Another alternative would be to use simple stone ornaments on plinths or trellis obelisks with climbing plants. The number of sentinels could be increased by treating the cross-axis path in the same way as the main path, but symmetrical grouping is essential.

HEDGES

The yew hedges are only waist high, so light is not restricted in the beds and the surrounding woodland becomes part of the garden design. A taller hedge would shade the beds, affecting what could be grown. The rectangularity of the hedges makes a pleasing foil to the planting, but topiary pilasters and corner bastions could add interest in winter. An evergreen hedge is essential for the design, and yew is by far the best material to use. It would reach this height in about five years. Thuja would be a satisfactory alternative, but Leyland cypress or privet should be avoided, as their coarseness would detract from this exquisite scene.

CROSS AXIS (*above*)

The view across the garden is framed by a wooden tunnel that is planted with roses, honeysuckle and late-flowering clematis. A complementary tableau - perhaps taking the form of a garden seat or another vase – at the far end would add importance to the vista.

THE PLANTING

This garden endures long hard winters, but from the moment spring arrives, a succession of flower tableaux provide bloom until well into the autumn. A foundation planting of shrubs and perennials is underplanted with drifts of bulbs for spring and summer, and ends with a finale of chrysanthemums.

Mirror-planting along the paths is supported by an informal balance of planting throughout the garden. It is a less labour-intensive scheme than it first appears because it is so thickly planted and also has a sprinkler system, so feeding, dead-heading, cutting back and some weeding are all that are required during the growing season. In the autumn most plants, except roses, hydrangeas and woody plants that may suffer winter burn, are cut back, and those plants that require winter protection are wrapped in plastic sheeting. In spring the rest of the pruning is done, and the entire garden is mulched with really good compost. From time to time, plants are discarded, replaced or divided, and the bulbs are topped up every few years.

Above Spring tulips include pink Lily-flowered 'Maytime', 'White Triumphator' and double-flowered 'Angelique'.

Above The north-west quadrant in summer includes yellow lilies, white phlox, deep pink spires of lythrum and grey *Stachys byzantina*, while the spiraea, tall yuccas and delphiniums are also in bloom.

SOUTH-WEST QUADRANT
1 *Chrysanthemum nipponicum* in late spring gives way to peonies, roses, astilbes and delphiniums in summer.
2 A swathe of different kinds of tulips makes way for more peonies, roses and phlox, and the flowering seasonr comes to an end with chrysanthemums.
3 *Iris germanica* and stachys line the path to the gazebo.
4 Buddleja.
5 More tulips are followed by astilbe, lupins, phlox, drifts of lilies, and chrysanthemums.
6 Roses and peonies are interplanted with lilies.
7 Juniper sentinels.
8 Iris and hyacinths, lavender, stachys and, later, sweet Williams along the path, are backed by peonies, lilies and roses.
9 Tradescantia and chrysanthemums (grown as annuals) line the path.
10 A standard white wisteria.

NORTH-WEST QUADRANT
11 Roses are interplanted with tall alliums and delphiniums.
12 Tulips make way for peonies, roses, purple loosestrife, a swathe of lilies, and finally chrysanthemums.
13 More peonies and roses take over from tulips, and are joined later by veronica, lilies and chrysanthemums.
14 A yucca stands high above other planting.
15 *Spiraea japonica* 'Anthony Waterer'.
16 Peonies line the hedge and provide a background for other planting.

17 Tulips are followed by baptisia, peonies, veronica, roses, purple loosestrife and chrysanthemums.
18 In spring, hyacinths and iris line the path; at the end of the summer, stachys, lavender and pansies are augmented by the appearance of chrysanthemums.

NORTH-EAST QUADRANT
19 Hyacinths, and later stachys and lavender along the central path are backed by peonies and roses and astilbes.
20 A tree peony (*Paeonia suffruticosa* 'Holiday').
21 Roses against the hedge are underplanted with *Iris ensata* (syn.*I. kaempferi*).
22 Swathes of tulips in spring give way to aquilegias, irises, astilbes,

roses, a mass of lilies, and finally chrysanthemums.
23 Standard 'French Lace' roses are surrounded with tulips, aquilegias, foxgloves and lilies.
24 Hyacinths and *Andromeda polifolia* 'Compacta' line the path.
25 An antique bird house stands in the corner.

SOUTH-EAST QUADRANT
26 A hydrangea makes a bold statement and is surrounded by roses.
27 A mass of tulips is followed by aquilegias, peonies, roses, echinops and many lilies.
28 Hyacinths along the circular path are followed by lavender and chrysanthemums.
29 Tulips are planted behind roses and peonies, and infilled with late chrysanthemums.

POOLSIDE
30 Planting includes lavender, roses, iberis, phlox, hinoki cypress and sedums, followed by chrysanthemums.

GAZEBO
31 Climbing roses include 'Madame Grégoire Staechelin', 'New Dawn' and 'First Prize'.

ARCH
32 Climbers include: *Rosa* 'Madame Grégoire Staechelin', *Lonicera*

periclymenum 'Serotina' and *Clematis flammula*.

33 A yew (*Taxus baccata*) hedge encloses the garden. Its annual clipping is made easier because it is only waist high.

PLANTS
The colour in the garden is orchestrated so that it changes subtly from bed to bed. Some of the plants appear in two, three, or all four of the quadrants, bringing a feeling of harmony to the garden. Astilbes include 'Bergkristall', 'Bridal Veil' and 'Peach Blossom'. Chrysanthemums include 'Grenadine', 'Cherish', 'Chiffon', 'Matador', 'Minnehaha', 'Prom Queen', 'Vulcan' and 'White Grandchild'. Hyacinths include *H. orientalis* 'Amethyst' 'Carnegie', 'City of Haarlem', 'Delft Blue', 'Gypsy Queen' and 'Lady Derby'. Bearded Iris cultivars include 'Charm Song', 'Elysian Fields', 'Grand Waltz', 'Harbor Blue', 'High Above', 'Loop the Loop', 'Mandolin', 'Peach Taffeta', 'South Pacific', 'Tenino', 'Triton' and 'Victoria Falls'. Lilies include *L. regale*, 'Black Dragon', Green Magic, 'Rosario', 'Star Gazer', African Queen, Imperial Silver and Imperial Gold. Peonies include *P. lactiflora* 'Mrs Livingstone

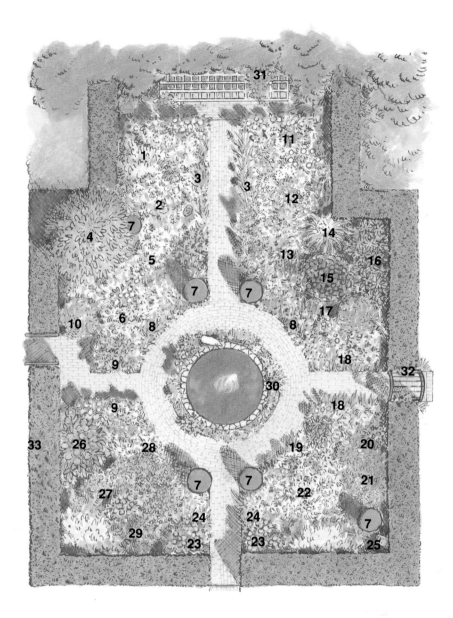

Farrand', 'Elsa Sass', 'Pillow Talk', 'Top Brass', 'Cheddar Cheese', 'Bowl of Cream', 'Bridal Gown', 'Chiffon Parfait', 'Monsieur Jules Elie', 'Raspberry Sundae'; tree peonies include *P. suffruticosa* 'Ariadne' and 'Holiday'. Phlox include *P.*

paniculata 'Bright Eyes', 'Dodo Hanbury Forbes', 'White Admiral' and *P. carolina* 'Miss Lingard'. Roses include 'Brandy', 'Garden Party', 'Honor', 'John F, Kennedy', Peace, 'Seashell', 'Sheer Bliss', 'Sonia', 'Summer Dream', 'Summer Fashion' and

'Tuxedo'. Tulips include 'Angélique', 'Balalaika', 'Ballade', 'Blue Parrot', 'Ivory Floradale', 'Maureen', 'Palestrina', 'Maytime', 'Pink Diamond', 'Queen of Night', 'Scotch Lassie', 'Shirley' and 'White Triumphator'.

OUTDOOR LIVING ROOMS

This is a garden blessed by a climate in which plants thrive and grow quickly and where there are no harsh winters. This means that a garden can be as much for living in as looking at. In this case the designer, Sonny Garcia, has excavated a steep hillside to create a pair of beautiful outdoor rooms, both of which form natural extensions to the house. The use of ceramic tiles, trickling water and the sense of inward-looking enclosure all spring from the patio tradition that travelled to the New World from Spain and Portugal. Here, however, a refreshing new strain has been grafted on to the time-hallowed stem in the form of the post-modernist latticework and gate together with the bronze sculptures of birds.

The initial cost of making this garden was very considerable because of the engineering involved in constructing the substantial retaining walls and because of the sheer quantity of good quality hard landscaping. Because the garden occupies vertical surfaces as well as ground space, it is more extensive than it might seem at first glance. Everything is seen at such close proximity that the garden needs a good deal of housekeeping. However, with electronically controlled systems for sprinklers and the pools, it will reward you with the perfect backdrop for outdoor entertaining for an investment of a regular afternoon's work each week, and an extra day or so every couple of months.

The use of hard surface materials – old, hand-made brick, terracotta and shiny ceramic tiles makes a pleasing contrast to the lush planting – a mix of formally trained evergreens, climbers and colourful perennials and annuals. The arch is entwined with fragrant *Mandevilla laxa* flanked by 'Peace', 'Mutabilis' and 'Graham Thomas' roses.

THE STRUCTURE

The garden measures about 15 x 9 m/50 x 30 ft overall. The 'dining room' is about 4.5 x 6 m/ 15 x 20 ft and the 'living room' is about 5.5 x 7.5 m/18 x 25 ft. The effect that the two main areas form 'rooms' depends very much on the enclosing walls, not one of which is less than about 2 m/6 ft high. The bold and unusual feature of this garden is the division of what might have been merely a long terrace next to the house into two distinct areas by

means of a small change in level and a semi-transparent wall and gate. If the space had been much smaller, it would have been possible to create only one 'room'. Although the terracing is an integral part of the scheme, it is not essential that it be quite so precipitous, or the walls so high – 1.2 m/4 ft would be sufficient to retain the effect of 'rooms', especially if the height was increased with planting or with trellis and climbers.

BRICK PAVING

Brick paving is always attractive, particularly old brick, or hand-made brick with an interesting patina (mass-produced bricks have a flat, unrelieved uniformity). In colder climes, bricks must be frost-resistant. The choice of brick for the 'floors' links these horizontals with the outer retaining walls. The warm colour is particularly appealing in a place where grey skies and sea mists are a regular feature of the

climate. In other situations, and especially where the architecture of the house might suggest it, alternative materials might be more

appropriate. As the garden is looked down on from the house, the pattern and effect of the 'flooring' must always be taken into consideration.

DINING ROOM *(left)*
The wall is broken by a pair of magnificent wooden doors that suggest another room beyond, but are, in fact, fake. The frieze and pedestal of yellow and blue tiles provide an

architectural unity to the area. Trellis on the walls on either side of the doors supports *Solanum jasminoides* 'Album'. The staircase behind the pedestal supports containers of shrubs and trailing variegated ivy.

WATER FEATURES
These add movement, sound and reflections but are extremely economical on space. The water is recycled through the masks, and the pool – ingeniously made more mysterious by running underneath a flight of steps – is kept clean by a filter system.

STEPS
Steps are a vital ingredient in a multi-level site. Here they are imaginatively sited to offer alternative routes to explore the garden, and the flights vary in length. The steps that arch over the pool are as dramatic as any stage setting: they act as a bridge; they are flanked by matching tiled wall panels whose centrepieces are ram's head wall fountains; and they are emphasized by paired containers of ivy topiary placed as accents on the bottom step. The functional flight of steps that leads from the 'dining room' to the terrace above serves as a vertical display surface for a series of trailing foliage plants.

ORNAMENTS (*above*)
A large terracotta pot and the wall plaque – a reproduction of a Renaissance ceramic by Della Robbia – makes an exceptionally effective focal point for the view from the dining area. The framing device of the gate, its curves echoed by the treillage above the plaque, adds further impact. Small garden ornaments are rarely satisfactory, even in a small space; simple additions that lend height or importance can work transformations – in this garden the pot adds scale to the small plaque – in the same way that the colourful tiled pedestal enhances the putto in the dining area.

THE PLANTING

The planting here falls into four distinct groups: the structural items including trees, shrubs and evergreens including topiary; the climbers and trailers for vertical interest; the container plants; and finally annuals and perennials. The first two groups provide the garden's backcloth which is embroidered by the others. It would be tempting to swamp the garden with strong colour, but instead it is furnished with an abundance of cooling greens, essential in a warm climate and a compensation for the absence of a lawn. Apart from the terrace, the planting is in close-focus and flaws easily detected, so the garden calls for year-round attention and the plants are occasionally replaced by pot-grown ones.

WIDE TERRACE BORDER
This is about 2.1 m/8 ft wide, and is filled with trees which normally grow to 13.5 m/40 ft or over, but which are kept severely pruned so that they do not over-dominate the site.
1 In the extreme corner there is an Australian tree fern (*Dicksonia antarctica*) and a wych elm (*Ulmus glabra* 'Camperdownii')
2 Flowering cherry (*Prunus* 'Shogetsu').

Right Passiflora 'Amethyst' is a deciduous climber with exotic purple flowers in summer followed by small green fruits.

Above The view of the terrace behind the pool provides contrasts of texture and form, living plants and man-made materials. The legs of the bird sculptures are echoed by the trunk of the prunus and the tall foxglove stems. *Felicia amelloides* breaks the line of the brick wall. In containers neat mounds of box contrast with a haze of *Helichrysum petiolare* 'Limelight'.

PONDSIDE BEDS

14 Herbs, including thyme and chives, and perennials including primulas and pinks have been chosen for their contrasting foliage as well as their flowers.

LATTICE WALL

15 The terracotta pot is surrounded with penstemons, *Berberis thunbergii* 'Rose Glow' and *Nepeta* 'Six Hills Giant'.
16 On the lattice is a passion flower flanked by *Rosa* 'Golden Showers' and *Cotinus coggygria* 'Royal Purple'.

3 The underplanting is of clipped box domes and standard escallonias.

'DINING ROOM' WALL

4 Behind clipped box hedges in raised beds, the white potato vine (*Solanum jasminoides* 'Album') is trained on white trellis on either side of the large double doors.
5 Standard yellow lantana and *Helichrysum petiolare* 'Limelight' are planted in containers above the wall, edging the terrace path.

STAIRCASE WALL

6 The troughs that ascend the steps contain a mixture of plants including variegated *Pieris japonica*, *Fuchsia* 'Gartenmeister Bonstedt' and abutilons; while cascades of

variegated *Hedera helix* hang down the wall.

HOUSE WALL

7 A *Magnolia* 'Elizabeth' is tucked into the corner next to the steps that curl up to another door leading into the house. The narrow bed is planted with a changing display of annuals and container-grown perennials together with a *Brugmansia* 'Charles Grimaldi'.

GATE SCREEN

8 *Mandevilla laxa* climbs over the arch, while the gate is flanked by yellow *Rosa* 'Graham Thomas', scented, coppery yellow *R.* 'Mutabilis' and the light yellow Hybrid Tea *R.* 'Peace'.
9 On the 'dining room'

side there are clipped box hedges in containers.

NORTH TERRACE BORDER

10 This is about 1.8 m/5 ft wide and is planted with a second *Prunus* 'Shogetsu'.
11 Shrubs chosen for colour and shape – *Spiraea japonica* 'Goldflame', *Berberis thunbergii* 'Rose Glow' and *Lavatera thuringiaca*. The ornamental foliage of *Gunnera tinctoria* and flowers such as *Felicia amelloides* fill the gaps.

'SITTING ROOM' WALL

12 Clipped box, penstemons, *Brachyscome multifida*, lavender, saxifrage, lobelia and *Rosa* 'Handel' are planted above the wall

in containers that line the terrace path.
13 Clematis and *Solanum dulcamara* climb the wall behind the bench.

HOUSE STEPS

17 These are flanked by two square beds containing pyramids of box and clipped lavender.

Below Solanum jasminoides 'Album' is a semi-evergreen wall shrub whose flowers are followed by purple berries.

A VISTA GARDEN

There is a welcoming luxuriance combined with a real sense of style about this garden. This clever solution to the perennial problem of the long narrow town back garden is a classic demonstration of the importance of contrasting ground level surfaces: soft verdant grass, crunchy caramel gravel and pale regular paving. Placing these elements in sequence subtly emphasizes the garden's width, and the staggered arrangement of the two small lawns is a more exciting use of space than a predictable central panel. Vertical accents and climbers are also vital elements in the garden's success. The surrounding fence provides privacy through supporting an almost year-round display of flower, and the pergola arch not only divides the space but delightfully frames two enchanting vistas.

Designed by Judith Sharpe, this garden belongs to the tradition of strong structure and luxuriant planting epitomized by the partnership at the turn of the century of Sir Edwin Lutyens, the architect, and Gertrude Jekyll, the plantswoman. The charm of this style is the way the natural forms of the plants blur and soften the underlying geometry of the layout. In terms of maintenance this presents a double challenge for gardeners: they must keep the plants in flourishing health to provide the impression of luxuriance, but at the same time unobtrusively groom and control their growth so that the result is exuberance rather than muddle.

The main vista to and from the house is off-centre and provides a strong axis connecting three different areas: an upper terrace providing a backcloth of shrubs and small trees; a formal garden with the sundial as a focal point; and a lawn that leads to a paved terrace next to the house.

STRUCTURE

This garden measures 23 x 6.5 m/75 x 21 ft. The principles of this design are ideal for a long narrow site such as this: the division across the width, and the creation of a sequence of contrasting gardens. The most important single element is the vista running from a viewpoint in the house through an arch to a sundial and on to a flight of steps which ascend into an illusory tangle of greenery. The sequence and contrast of grass, gravel and paving is another key to its success, providing interesting variations in terms of colour and surface texture. Although the three gardens are separately defined areas, their essential unity is emphasized by an overall colour control running through the whole scheme, progressing through pinks to lavender, lilac and purple.

PAVING

A terrace provides transitional area between house and garden, one in which to sit and place containers. The paving here is of regular slabs, low key and unobtrusive. Always choose paving in tones and materials that harmonize with those of the building. A combination of plain flagstones with details in old brick, setts or cobbles is often attractive, but more expensive to buy and to lay than plain slabs.

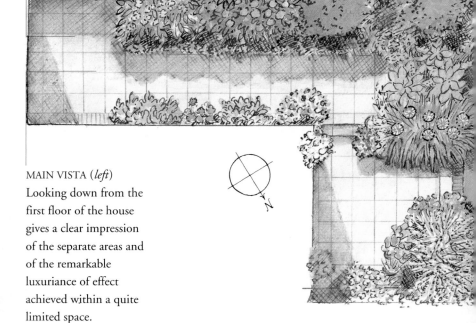

MAIN VISTA (*left*)
Looking down from the first floor of the house gives a clear impression of the separate areas and of the remarkable luxuriance of effect achieved within a quite limited space.

TRELLIS

The enclosing wooden fences on two sides have been topped with sturdy trellis treated with wood preservative. Cheap trellis is a false economy. It should be of good quality and treated with preservative to minimize maintenance. Even so, it is a relatively economical way of creating transparent garden screens, in this case adding to privacy and providing support for an explosion of foliage and bloom. It adds aerial architecture which responds to the interplay of light, casting a lattice-work of shadows onto the ground.

BOX HEDGE

This is the most important of the few elements of green architecture in the garden. Box, with its small glossy leaves, compact habit and pungency, is not as slow-growing as many people imagine, but the length of hedge here is so short that it would be well worth purchasing large plants for an immediate effect. It requires at the most two clippings a year to keep it immaculate, and an annual feeding of bonemeal. Euonymus or *Lonicera nitida* would be possible alternatives, though both need more attention than box.

SERVICE AREA SHRUBBERY

Terracing what would have been a gently sloping site into two distinct levels adds an extra dimension to the garden. This cleverly adds to the illusion of the size of the garden at the same time as providing space for a shed for garden tools. Trees and shrubs on being planted immediately look larger if they are on a raised terrace, and the wall allows for a display of prostrate plants. Care must be taken that the earth is held in on all four sides by retaining walls. Here it has a weed-suppressing mulch of wood chips, but an alternative would be paving. The introduction of a very simple bench or seat from which to enjoy the garden's main vista back to the house would be an attractive addition.

PERGOLA ARCH

A beautifully sited simple framing device like this draws and focuses the eye on the sundial beyond. In such a small space it is not only a perfect support for a display of all kinds of climbers but is the crucial architectural structure dividing the garden. There are any number of ready-manufactured arches available from simple larchwood to elaborate Victorian-style ironwork ones, but it is often just as economical to get a local blacksmith to make one to your chosen dimensions. If you opt for timber, be sure that the wood has been properly treated with preservative. Whatever it is made from, make it large enough so that, once smothered with greenery, it can still be walked through and retain its role as a frame; and be sure that it is strong enough to carry the weight of the plants. Remember, too, in siting it that it frames the view both ways.

THE PLANTING

There is a classic, country-house quality to the planting of this garden. It is an orchestration of much-loved flowering shrubs, perennials, roses and climbers. It is often a good idea to use a restricted palette of colour in a small space and here the colour is limited to a range of pinks, blues and purples with an occasional burst of white. Grey and silver foliage plants add a pleasing counterpoint. Careful consideration has been given to the two main borders: the resulting effect is luxuriant for what is a fairly modest input of labour. It is the lawn which is the most taxing commitment during the mowing season, but small areas like this so close to the house would be ideal candidates for lightweight, electric mowers. There are no annuals except those introduced in containers. The perennials would benefit from some regular grooming to remove fading leaves, and some staking during the growing season, but little serious attention. They call for mulching and feeding each year, and then lifting and dividing every few years. The climbers need tying-in and dead-heading during the growing season, and each requires annual pruning. In general, once the plants have established themselves, the main problem will be to check their prolific and potentially invasive growth.

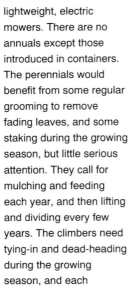

NARROW SHADY TERRACE
1 Against the wall and trellis are *Hydrangea anomala petiolaris*, *Lonicera periclymenum* 'Belgica' and *Clematis montana rubens*.
2 In the bed are *Viburnum davidii*, *Hydrangea macrophylla*, *Helleborus foetidus*, hostas and *Viburnum tinus*.

TERRACE CONTAINERS
3 The planting varies from year to year but usually includes *Hedera helix* 'Glacier' and *Helichrysum italicum microphyllum*, and a range of pink, blue-grey and white flowers such as ivy-leaved geraniums, lobelia, petunias, impatiens, nicotiana, trailing *Verbena x hybrida* 'Sissinghurst' and *Nolana* 'Bluebird'.

SOUTH BORDER
4 This is anchored with a *Rhus typhina* underplanted with *Bergenia cordifolia*.
5 Other plants include *Euphorbia characias wulfenii* and hostas.
6 *Cotinus coggygria* 'Royal Purple', *Abelia x grandiflora*, *Eucalyptus gunnii* (stooled), and *Ceanothus thyrsiflorus repens*, with *Stachys byzantina*, *Sedum telephium maximum* 'Atropurpureum' and

Below Viticella clematis 'Minuet' is a late-flowering, fully hardy variety that does not require pruning.

Below Narcissus triandrus, a bulb which naturalizes beneath deciduous trees, has long-lasting flowers.

'Maidwell Hall', *Rosa* 'Variegata di Bologna' and *Rosa* 'New Dawn' provide bloom from spring to summer.

NORTH BORDER
14 *Acanthus spinosus*, hostas and sedums are paired with those in the opposite border.
15 *Rosa* 'Roseraie de L'Haÿ' and *R.* 'Penelope' are planted behind *Alchemilla mollis* and *Lavandula angustifolia*.
16 *Amelanchier lamarckii* is underplanted with *Iris*

'Jane Philips', *Astrantia major*, *Viola cornuta* and *V.c.* Alba Group.
17 *Rosa* 'Reine des Violettes' and Viticella clematis 'Minuet' clothe the trellis.
18 *Cotinus coggygria* 'Royal Purple' and *Berberis thunbergii atropurpurea* grows behind lavender and artemisia.

SOUTH WALL AND TRELLIS
19 *Clematis* 'Marie Boisselot' and *Rosa* 'Mme Grégoire Staechelin'.

20 *Lonicera periclymenum* 'Serotina'.
21 *Rosa* 'Mme Alfred Carriere'.

RAISED SERVICE AREA
22 Pots of nicotiana and lobelia cascade down the wall.
23 *Hedera canariensis* 'Gloire de Marengo' and *Clematis montana* 'Elizabeth' cover the shed.
24 *Eucalyptus pauciflora niphophila*.
25 *Pyrus salicifolia* 'Pendula' is underplanted with spring-flowering

white narcissus including *N.* 'Ice Follies' and *N.* 'Mount Hood'.
26 Pots of agaves stand sentinel on the steps.

Below The view from the lawn nearest the house looks over *Anemone* x *hybrida* and *Acanthus spinosus* towards the retaining wall at the far end of the garden.

ajuga in front.
7 *Parthenocissus henryana*, *Clematis* 'Perle d'Azur' and *C.* 'Comtesse de Bouchaud' clothe the trellis.
8 *Hydrangea macrophylla*.
9 The arm of the border is filled with *Eryngium variifolium*, *Anemone* x *hybrida*, *Sedum* 'Autumn Joy', *Acanthus spinosus*, *Polygonum affine* and hostas.

PERGOLA ARCH
10 *Clematis* 'Perle d'Azur' and *Rosa mulliganii* climb over the arch, while nepeta grows at their feet.

SMALL RAISED BEDS
Two slightly raised beds contain sun-loving plants.
11 Agapanthus.
12 *Teucrium fruticans*.

NORTH WALL AND TRELLIS
13 *Clematis macropetala*

Left An abstract contemporary sculpture is the garden's focal point. The view towards the brilliantly coloured fencing is softened by the spiky leaves of *Miscanthus sinensis* 'Strictus' and the feathery branches of *Fargesia murieliae.*

Right Painted grey-blue, the bridge which crosses the garden ponds makes a strong contrast to the horizontal red fencing. A bold clump of *Typha latifolia* provides a vertical feature among aquatic marginals which include *Pontedaria cordata.*

This is a garden to satisfy the most ambitious. It boldly sweeps away conventional notions about water in the garden – which usually takes the form of small geometric or irregular pools, cascades or fountains – in favour of an aquatic totality. The garden in this instance *is* water. Essentially, it is two large water-filled containers; its boundaries are evergreen hedging or brightly-coloured fences of slatted wood, and its paths are wooden bridges crossing the water leaving just enough space for beds for water-loving plants at the edges.

This is a refreshing, one might say almost breath-taking extravaganza whose construction could never be anything other than professional and expensive. However, it is money well spent, for, once installed and planted, it requires astoundingly little maintenance during the growing season. The ponds have a sophisticated filter system and the beds and borders are skilfully planted in soil whose type and moisture content have been artificially manipulated by the designer, Henk Weijers.

The result, however, is a unique, indeed thrilling garden experience owing nothing to nostalgia. The bold, almost brutal, rectangularity of the defining enclosures is offset by a lush exuberance of planting, huge drifts of marsh marigolds, spikes of pickerel weed and clumps of bamboo. What is so innovative about this water garden is its deliberate avoidance of phoney naturalistic effects such as artificial waterfalls or irregular edgings of rock. Instead it triumphantly celebrates its own artifice as the work of man.

AN INNOVATIVE WATER GARDEN

DECKING WALKS

The handsome decking provides the walkway linking the north and south terraces. Decking should always be made of high quality seasoned and treated timber. The biggest drawback of wood is that it can prove slippery, particularly in a wet climate. In another setting this pathway could be constructed of stone, brick or setts, or a mixture. If this decision is made it would be important that its design should not be nostalgic but of our own time.

RAISED BORDER (*left*)

The narrow raised border edging the second pond is filled with herbaceous plants, among them orange-yellow *Hemerocallis* hybrid, violet *Scabiosa caucasica* and the dark carmine *Geranium sanguineum*.

The decking walkway on two levels divides the two ponds. On one side there are water marginals *Pontederia cordata* and *Sagittaria sagittifolia*, and on the other side is a huge fountain of *Miscanthus floridulus* foliage.

THE STRUCTURE

The site overall measures roughly 18 x 15 m/60 x 50 ft and is held in by a timber fence on two sides and part of a third, the rest being an evergreen thuja backing hedge running the width of the garden. Within these confines the design is abstract: angular areas of water, decking, planting and terrace at two different levels forming, if seen from above, something akin to a canvas by the painter Mondrian. The essence of the design is the clear demarcation of what are a series of sharply differentiated textures and colours: black reflective water, ribbed shiny wooden decking, stone paved terraces, brightly coloured fencing and beds filled with greenery flecked with flowers. The abrupt juxtaposition of these elements heightens the drama: one pond forms an L-shape outside the living room, bringing water to lap at the foot of a full-length window. Although strikingly of our own time, this garden belongs to the centuries-old tradition of the formal water parterre. Here water has taken the place normally accorded in a garden to grass, forming static mirrors reflecting light at ground level and giving opportunities for planting marginals and aquatics. Although at first sight dramatic, the ponds are, in fact, quite shallow. (However, it is unwise to incorporate even shallow water features in a garden scheme where young children may be present.) The principles of the scheme are adaptable to any flat rectangular site. One pond with its surrounding decking and beds could form either a small garden in itself or be introduced as part of a larger different scheme. Such a composition calls for professional landscaping, although a scaled-down version could well be with reach of an exceptionally capable handyman, provided expert help was sought for the technicalities of plumbing and drainage.

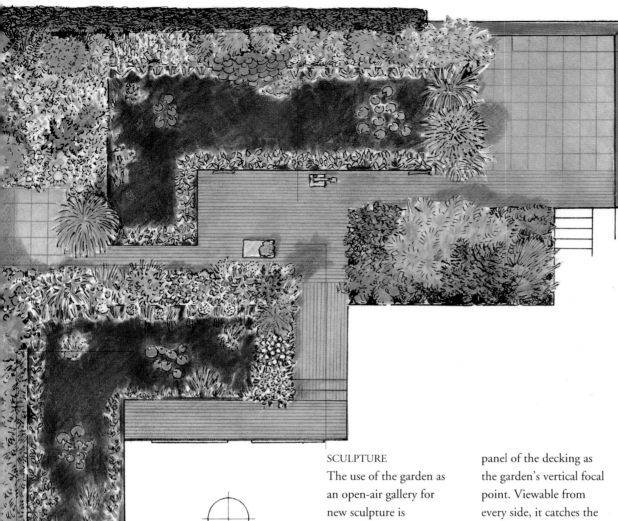

FENCING

Generally not enough use is made of strong colour on the hard built surfaces of today's gardens. This brilliant exception takes its scarlet hue from part of the central sculpture and emphasizes the south-facing terrace. It is deliberately done as a bold vertical statement with no attempt to age the surface or to cover or soften it with climbers. Its horizontal linearity echoes the planking in the decking. Bright blue would be almost as arresting, but not yellow as so many of the flowers are that colour, and yellow is too close to the light greens of much of the foliage.

SCULPTURE

The use of the garden as an open-air gallery for new sculpture is exhilarating. An abstract contemporary piece is placed on the central panel of the decking as the garden's vertical focal point. Viewable from every side, it catches the light and echoes the primary colours of the fencing and flowers.

PONDS

These are not so much ponds as shallow tanks in which to grow plants. They are lined with black flexible polythene sheeting (Butyl is the strongest and most expensive). Another solution would be to have them constructed of concrete. The first fillings of water will be cloudy due to the concrete exuding lime, and the pond will need emptying and refilling until the water begins to 'green up', indicating that algae can survive in it. This process can take some months, though pond sealers will short-cut the procedure. This garden is equipped with an electrically operated filter system to maintain the best possible water conditions and to prevent the ponds from freezing. Filter systems are a worthwhile investment for a garden that relies on its water effects. Late autumn care will demand the raking out of fallen leaves and plant debris unless the water has wire netting placed over it.

Left The narrow border is filled with violet blue *Scabiosa caucasica* and orange *Hemerocallis* hybrid. Against the hedge arise spikes of *Ligularia* 'The Rocket'. Behind the large bush of *Miscanthus floridulus* there is the *Liquidambar styraciflua*, whose leaves turn claret-red in autumn.

THE PLANTING

The designer has little sympathy for evergreens as they only provide one effect and he prefers deciduous plants which during any year will provide a succession of pictures from bare branches onwards. A careful selection of these, set against an evergreen thuya hedge, makes a backcloth framing the two ponds. As a consequence, for people who do not share this viewpoint, the garden would seem to be chiefly a summertime one. There is some provision for winter, spring and autumn interest in some of the shrubs and trees, the *Viburnum tinus* and *V. farreri*, *Prunus fruticosa* 'Globosa' and *Liquidambar styraciflua*.

But in the main both borders and ponds come to life from the late spring. One exciting aspect of such an 'unnatural' water garden is that no lipservice needs to be paid to the convention of appropriate waterside planting. The beds and borders are artificial environments and their soil type and moisture content are for the gardener to determine. Many of the beds call for weeding and regular general attention such as dead-heading; and perennials will need periodic division. This could be achieved by running a gantry over the water. Once or twice a year the beds need to be judiciously invaded to clip the hedge and prune the shrubs.

POND PLANTS

All these need to be planted in round or square perforated plastic containers of a kind easily obtainable from any garden centre. Different plants call for different sizes. The containers will need to be lined with sacking to prevent soil from seeping into the water. At the bottom should be placed some

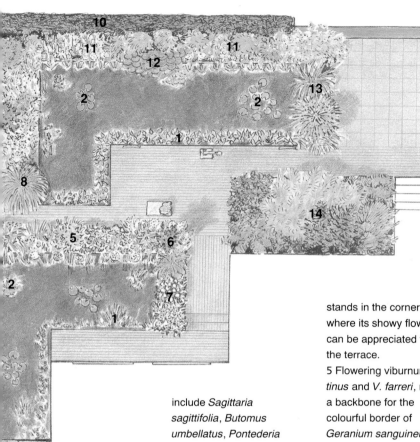

well-rotted compost, then medium heavy clay soil and finally small stones to protect the plant's root system. Check the depth at which each plant should be positioned and support it, if necessary beneath with blocks or bricks.Periodic division of the aquatics and marginals – every two or three years – is made easier by simply lifting the planting containers, which also restrict these potentially invasive plants.
1 The marginal plants include *Sagittaria sagittifolia*, *Butomus umbellatus*, *Pontederia cordata*, *Typha angustifolia* and *Alisma plantago-aquatica*.
2 The aquatic plants include *Nymphaea alba* and *N. odorata rosea*, *Ranunculus aquatilis*, *Mentha aquatica*, *Stratiotes aloides* and *Utricularia vulgaris*.

SHORTER POND BORDERS
3 A screening of *Yushania anceps* (syn. *Arundinaria jaunsarensis*) along the south border also includes *Prunus laurocerasus* 'Schipkaensis' and is interplanted with *Euphorbia myrsinites* and *Ligularia przewalskii*.
4 *Weigela* 'Newport Red'

stands in the corner where its showy flowers can be appreciated from the terrace.
5 Flowering viburnums, *V. tinus* and *V. farreri*, make a backbone for the colourful border of *Geranium sanguineum*, *Hemerocallis* hybrid and *Scabiosa caucasica*.
6 *Nothofagus antarctica* marks the turn of the border.
7 *Viburnum tinus*, *Asplenium trichomanes*, *Prunella grandiflora* and *Incarvillea delavayi* fill the northern arm of the border.

LONGER POND BORDERS
8 *Miscanthus floridulus* makes a major statement.
9 The wall border has a foundation of trees and shrubs including *Liquid-ambar styraciflua* and *Cercidiphyllum japonicum* whose leaves contribute brilliant autumn colour,

evergreen spring-flowering *Prunus laurocerasus* 'Schipkaensis' and *Viburnum* 'Pragense' and *Prunus fruticosa* 'Globosa' and *Viburnum* x *burkwoodii*. All will need pruning to keep them restricted in size. Between and under these is a range of perennials and shrubs including *Lysimachia nummularia*, *Pleioblastus humilis pumilus*, *Heuchera* x *brizoides*, *Geranium endressii* 'Wargrave Pink',*Waldsteinia geoides*, *Lysimachia punctata*, *L. clethroides*, *Polygonatum* x *hybridum* and *Asplenium scolopendrium*.
10 An evergreen hedge of thuja screens the west boundary.
11 The long narrow border beneath the hedge

is planted with *Polygonatum* x *hybridum*, *Ligularia* 'The Rocket', *Lythrum salicaria* 'Robert', *Fargesia murieliae*, *Lysimachia nummularia*, *Anemone tomentosa* 'Robustissima', *Ligularia dentata*, *Asarum europaeum,* and *Astilbe* 'Rheinland'.
12 *Petasites japonicus* dominates the middle portion of the bed.
13 *Iris germanica* and *Fargesia murieliae* make the most impact in the northern arm of the border, and are in-filled with *Tradescantia* 'Innocence', *Miscanthus sinensis, Fragaria vesca* and *Astilbe* 'Rheinland'.

EVERGREEN BORDER
14 This substantial screening border is filled with a mixture of junipers, pines, mahonia and ivy.

Below *Euphorbia myrsinites* is a useful low evergreen prostrate perennial with bright clusters of flowers in spring

A COURTYARD MAZE

This is a garden for flower and herb lovers that is equally satisfying to those who appreciate evergreen structure. Two rectangular mazes are articulated by bold hedges of shiny leaved green box and held in by an aerial tapestry of trained hornbeam. Three tall fruit trees spread their branches over two connecting courtyards which have been transformed into a plant-lovers' paradise. The herb garden brings with it the tradition of centuries, each plant endowed with its special properties. Its gentle tonality forms a striking prelude to the luxuriant galaxy of colour in the flower garden.

What is so striking about this garden, designed by André van Wassenhove, is its sense of control. The rectangularity of the hedging makes a brilliant counterfoil to the carefully orchestrated disarray of the plants, which are grouped according to their preference for sun or shade. The green box compensates visually for the lack of lawn and also eliminates the repetitive boredom of regular mowing. This releases the owners to direct their energies towards maintaining the beds of herbaceous plants which are their passion and which include an impressive array of interesting plants. These will call for constant but infinitely rewarding attention. Two good mornings or afternoons a week could be spent sustaining such horticultural glory, but less time would be needed if you chose undemanding ground-cover plants and slower-growing shrubs in place of the flowering perennials.

THE STRUCTURE

These are essentially two quite separate gardens, visually linked because both are designed according to the same principles. The inner herb garden is about 12 x 9 m/40 x 30 ft. The outer main flower garden about 17 x 10 m/50 x 34 ft. Both are paved with setts outlining a carefully balanced asymmetrical arrangement of rectangular beds of different sizes. The ancestors of the composition are the parterres and mazes of the seventeenth century, here reinterpreted in terms of twentieth-century abstract art. One of the charms of this design is the open-ended 'U' and 'L' shapes made by the box hedging: the closed squares and rectangles traditionally used to edge beds have a more predictable, heavier effect and are less easy to tend. The hard surfaces, which are undemanding to maintain, allow ease of access to all areas of the garden and provide three delightful areas in which to sit. This design is adaptable to any flat site – and, indeed, the herb garden usefully provides an alternative for a smaller flower garden – although particular care would be needed to ensure that the individual blocks and beds added up to a pattern that made a satisfying overall effect.

AERIAL HEDGE

Pleached hedges can be made out of lime, or, as here, of hornbeam. The young trees need a strong framework of supports – battens, wires or bamboo canes on which to train the lateral branches. You will need access in late summer or winter for the pruning and training. Hornbeam is particularly good because the pliable young growth is easy to tie in and pruning results in a dense, twiggy mass which provides privacy and filters wind. It adds to the green elements in summer and provides an intriguing pattern of entwining branches against the sky in winter.

FRUIT TREES
Here three fruit trees add height to what is an essentially low-level composition; they also provide shade, and attractive shadow patterns. The tradition of including fruit trees in a flower garden is very old. Pollination is needed for fruiting: you need compatible varieties or (for a single tree) a self-fertile type. An alternative might be small ornamental trees that produce blossom and then either berries or good autumn foliage, as they need less attention than fruit trees.

FISH POND
Water brings light, movement and the chance to plant aquatics and marginals. The spread of the plants in this pool has to be checked each year. A less labour-intensive alternative would be to omit both fish and planting and opt for water with a simple jet, or to replace it with a bed of the same proportions.

CLIPPED BOX
The introduction of square 'cushions' of box is an ingenious means of making up for the absence of lawn, which normally provides year-round ground-level green. The box hedging provides interest as light and shade articulate its square-cut shapes. The full impact of a parterre or maze is, however revealed only from above. It is from the upstairs windows of the house that the definite ground patterns are best enjoyed.

CONSERVATORY (*right*)
The newly constructed conservatory looks over a dining terrace into the flower garden. To the left the long aerial hedge of hornbeam ensures privacy and shelter.

PLANTING

This is a garden with an abundance of herbs and hardy herbaceous perennials. Nearly all call for attention, certainly in terms of lifting and dividing alone. As this only needs to be done about every five years, one way of coping would be to stagger the task and establish a rota of replanting one or two beds a year. The flower garden includes many plants like delphiniums which demand staking. In addition, to achieve a dazzling display all beds must be annually fed at least with bonemeal or some general purpose fertilizer, but better still with compost and farmyard manure. This is essentially a spring through autumn planting with the main display during the summer months; however, the box provides permanent green framing. To look immaculate, the box may sometimes need clipping twice a year. Anyone embarking on such a garden would wish to make their own scheme, maybe one which would include roses and even a few annuals. Any scheme, however, must be guided by the disposition of the site, with sun-loving plants at one end graduating to those which tolerate shade. Consideration

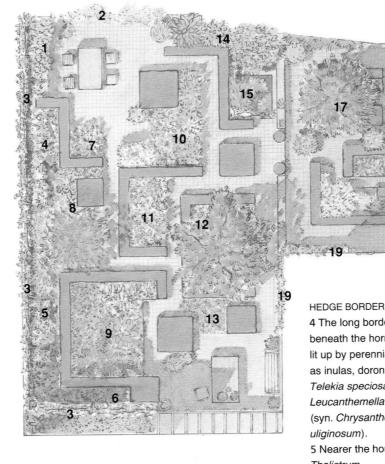

here has also been given to arrangement according to height, so that each large bed has a group of flowers with spikes of bloom which arise above the green hedge. An apple, a pear and a mulberry contribute spring blossom as well as fruit. The pruning of fruit trees calls for considerable skill. The techniques are best learned from an expert or at the least from a careful study of pruning manuals with good diagrams. Bad pruning can not only

disfigure the tree but reduces its capacity to produce fruit.

TERRACE WALLS
1 The bold foliage of *Macleaya cordata* forms a backdrop to the dining area.
2 *Wisteria sinensis* clothes the adjacent wall.

AERIAL HEDGE
3 Pleached hornbeam (*Carpinus betulus*) makes an airy overhead screen along the north and west boundaries.

HEDGE BORDER
4 The long border beneath the hornbeams is lit up by perennials such as inulas, doronicums, *Telekia speciosa* and *Leucanthemella serotina* (syn. *Chrysanthemum uliginosum*).
5 Nearer the house are *Thalictrum rochebrunanum*, *Cimicifuga racemosa* and *Phlomis russeliana*.
6 The shady corner includes *Hosta rectifolia* 'Tall Boy', *Polystichum setiferum* and *Glechoma hederacea*.

SMALL TERRACE BED
7 *Acanthus hungaricus* (syn. *A. longifolius*) is underplanted with *Prunella grandiflora* and *Thymus serpyllum albus*.

APPLE TREE BED
8 This small bed contains

Delphinium Summer Skies Group, *Phlomis russeliana* and *Meconopsis cambrica*.

LARGE SHADY BED
9 The principal plants are *Cimicifuga simplex* 'White Pearl', *Osmunda regalis* and *Hosta fortunei hyacinthina*, underplanted by *Glechoma hederacea*.

LARGE TERRACE BED
10 This sunny bed includes *Anaphalis triplinervis*, *Chelone obliqua*, *Dianthus* 'Duchess of Fife', *Gypsophila paniculata* 'Rosenschlier', *Malva alcea*, *Nepeta mussinii*, *Oenothera macrocarpa* and *Phlox paniculata* 'Lilac Time'.

SMALL CENTRAL BED
11 *Helleborus orientalis* is followed by *Delphinium*

'Völkerfrieden', *Gillenia trifoliata*, *Phlox paniculata* 'White Admiral' and *Sedum spectabile*.

PEAR TREE BED

12 Under the canopy grow *Brunnera macrophylla*, *Geranium endressii*, *Sidalcea candida*, *Ophiopogon japonicus*, *Anemone* x *hybrida* 'Honorine Jobert' and *Cimicifuga racemosa*. Nearby are *Delphinium* x *belladonna* 'Cliveden Beauty' and *Phlox paniculata* 'Rijnstroom'.

COURTYARD BED

13 Planting here includes *Dicentra formosa* 'Stuart Boothman', wolfsbane (*Aconitum pyrenaicum*) and *Rheum palmatum*, with *Liriope muscari*, *Lysimachia nummularia* and *Ajuga pyramidalis*.

POND AREA

14 *Crambe cordifolia*, *Persicaria amplexicaulis* *Cephalaria gigantea* and *Darmera peltata* grow with a fig tree.
15 Iris and waterlilies thrive in the pond.

HERB GARDEN

16 A range of herbs, not all culinary, is planted randomly in the beds with some ornamentals. Pots of standard fuchsias punctuate the design.
17 The specimen tree here is a white mulberry (*Morus alba*).
18 This wall is clothed with *Fallopia sachalinensis*.
19 *Parthenocissus tricuspidata* 'Veitchii', which contributes good autumn colour, climbs on several walls.

Above Malva alcea, is a substantial structural free-flowering perennial.

Left A view from the herb garden looks towards the far wall of the flower garden and the aerial hedge. Tall iris foliage rises from the pond to the right, and beyond that is the south-facing terrace with chairs and table backed by the blue-grey foliage of tall *Macleaya cordata*. To the left the branches of the apple tree spread a leafy canopy over the display of flowers below.

GARDENS
for the
ENTHUSIAST

Left This simple garden avoids the cliché of a large central lawn by using grass as a foil and a frame for a circular, generously scaled flowerbed. As it is the crisp edging rather than any structure that defines the bed, regular upkeep is essential. Its shape, echoed by the raised central section, and the simple brick path are what will give this bed its winter interest. Other gardeners might add a central focal point such as a sundial or an urn, but the massed mixed planting of perennials used here is in keeping with its surroundings.

*Previous page*s An herbaceous border at its apogee is a crowning achievement of garden art – but one reserved for the dedicated gardener. Roses and mallows form the backdrop for a range of shrubs and perennials that include spreaders and self-seeders. They are so densely planted that they support one another and do not need the more formal option of staking. The tumbling, casual effect is deceptive: keeping a border looking as good as this is a major commitment.

There will always be people for whom gardening is a way of life, for whom each hour spent tending the garden is one to be treasured. The difference between them and those with less commitment and time is one of priorities. They will either have more time – or have decided to allocate more time – to spend on the garden. High-maintenance gardens call for year-long commitment in all weathers. Over the years the work involved will result in a sophistication of knowledge which links the hand wielding fork or trowel to the one taking a book from the shelf. Committed gardeners will be engrossed both physically and mentally in the garden. On the darkest winter evenings they will turn to garden writers for inspiration, information and sheer pleasure. They will usually be avid garden visitors, anxious to learn from others, and will join one of the many gardening societies to share their enthusiasm. Knowledge will bring speed and shortcuts. It will also open the doors to an even wider range of horticultural effects, in particular those obtained through pruning and training, and to the infinity of plants available through various methods of propagation. The enthusiast will first and foremost be a plantsman, for the more varieties and

Right Here a profusion of flowers flanks and encloses a path and lawn. Low edging plants build up in a sophisticated planning through medium-height perennials and shrubby plants to arching shrubs and species roses. The division of a garden into different 'compartments', however loosely, increases the number of viewpoints from which the planting would look good. The lawn and containers increase the work load, but also the overall effect.

the more exotic the plants, the more demanding the garden. Always, however, be honest about the depth of your commitment, for nothing is a sadder sight than a high-maintenance garden in the hands of a low-maintenance gardener.

If, therefore, gardening is to be your consuming passion, then every garden effect, within reason, can be yours. But you will still need to observe the principle of good structure: otherwise your horticultural paradise will descend into plant chaos. Just because your garden is filled with a breathtaking range of difficult-to-grow and obscure plants, it does not mean that you will have a good garden. In a small space, that collection needs to be orchestrated and held together by a strong framework to give it definition, identity and balance. The five different gardens here are successful because they observe that rule.

A rustic arbour and sowing of foxglove spikes provide the vertical accents in this crowded cottage-garden scene. Self-seeding poppies and foxgloves create random effects, but a sure eye has seen that purples, pinks and reds are in rich harmony with the permanent planting of deep pink roses and wine-red clematis festooning the arbour. The challenge for the gardener is that of unobtrusively keeping the profusion from lapsing into chaos.

They are all rich in plants, but equally all are held together by different structural design solutions which display these treasures to the highest advantage.

They include certain types of garden open only to the utterly committed, since their demands are so intensive. One is the plant collector's garden, an explosion of horticultural acquisitiveness and curiosity that again calls for a powerful underlying design to hold it in order as a composition. It is, of course, essential to establish the ideal habitat in which particular plants can thrive and multiply. A collection of snowdrops, for instance, will call for undisturbed shade and lavish applications of leaf mould, while grey foliage plants need sun and do best in light, sandy soil. You then need to work back from your plant passion and consider what structural features will set them off to greatest

A beautifully tended and orchestrated display of perennials and herbs, many of them neatly trained into compact rounded bushes echoing the rhythm of the paving and the simple focal point, a stone bowl filled with stones and water. Clipped box balls and standard euonymus add vital architectural structure to a carefully calculated planting with subtle colour contrasts ranging through the greys and grey-greens. Clipping is vital to keep shrubby herbs like helichrysum (or santolina), rue and lavender from becoming leggy, and the result is beautifully displayed in this well-groomed planting.

advantage, and how best to place them. Many plant-oriented gardeners have little time for the basic concepts of design. This is usually a mistake and often both the gardener and the plants are the losers. Many of the structural solutions presented in this book will accommodate plant collections and provide them with a sure framework in which to flourish and be seen at their best. Just as I have argued that virtually all the designs in the book can be adjusted to minimum labour input by simplifying the planting, the converse is also true: planting can as easily be enriched and elaborated.

A second is the potager, a glorious mixture of fruit, flowers and vegetables woven into a stunning composition. Unlike other gardens, it is closely related to another art, cooking. It would be pointless embarking on one without a keen and firm alliance with the practicalities of the kitchen and the cook. Its creator must pay keen attention not only to the realities of crop rotation, but also to the visual potential of the transitory juxtaposition of vegetable leaf shape and colour. Within its firm geometrical frame, the garden picture will be a different one every year. In that resides much of the excitement of the potager. Constant care and application is essential from the planting of the seeds to the harvesting of the produce. But the result is a rare horticultural masterpiece.

This tiny potager, like an oasis in a wilderness, and cobble-edged beds has an almost hallucinatory quality, yet its ingredients could not be more modest. The area is enclosed by rustic palings in keeping with natural surroundings but which are also functional in keeping hungry rabbits out. Inside, it is symmetrically divided and the cobble-edged beds are jammed with an inspiring mixture of edible and ornamental plants. Towering sunflowers (some not yet in flower), runner bean pyramids and massed nasturtiums blur the boundaries between useful and decorative kitchen-garden plants. Flowers like nicotiana, cleome and cosmos are there purely for decoration, but the scattering of French marigolds in the beds helps deter pests. Every aspect of the planting patently gives pleasure, from the gone-to-seed grasses (bottom left) to the glossy leaves of the ruby chard (top right), but the garden is obviously productive and practical. The narrow beds make cultivation easy.

The third type is the Japanese garden which no-one except the initiated should attempt. On first encounter Japenese gardens seem so austere that they appear artlessly simple. But in reality they rank as one of the most demanding of all garden types. They embody not only a style but a philosophy and the two are deeply entwined and both must be seriously studied. Every aspect is governed by strict underlying principles, from the orientation of the entire garden to the detailed siting and association of plants and artefacts.

Enthusiasts in the small garden will probably also wish to experiment with plant propagation using a small propagator in a greenhouse. They might indeed raise annuals from seed and hence be able to indulge in that ultimate extravaganza of bedding-out, which means a spring, summer and autumn planting in succession.

The passionate gardener will be someone with a habit of mind that enjoys the fundamentals of the craft. Tasks which many people find a drudge – gathering leaves for the compost heap, bending double for hours to hand-weed beds, rushing out to beat snow off branches about to break beneath the pressure, or the time-consuming monoto-

Right A fan-trained cherry tree is a work of art. It also solves the problem of a shady wall. The branches are trained onto a cane framework but it would take several years of patient work to achieve this effect. The formality of this tableau is emphasized by the containing box hedge and the flanking pillars of clipped pyracantha.

ny of mowing a lawn – each will bring to an enthusiast its own particular pleasure. But then the labour and the demands will be offset by the beauty which the gardener's vision has created.

More than anything else serious gardeners will read, and accumulate a library. They will wish to know in depth their craft, moving beyond the rudimentary approach to a garden as an area for profit and pleasure to understanding some of its deeper resonances. They will want to understand the thoughts and actions of the great gardeners and garden-makers through the centuries, and that can only come from books and visits on the ground. Gradually the garden will assume for them something more profound, a philosophy of life.

A PLANTSMAN'S FANTASY

Skilful changes of level, and planting of a jungle-like density combine to make this small town garden quite extraordinary. Its composition bespeaks a warm climate which makes both outdoor living and a year-round profusion of plants possible. This is not a garden formula that would work in more extreme climates, for its success depends on the sheer exuberance of foliage and flowers. A wide spectrum of leaf and flower colour is matched by strategic placing of plants with distinctive silhouettes and habits to make every part of the garden interesting. The owner, the garden designer Sonny Garcia, usually devotes two hours a day to tending his ever-growing collection of exotic plants, and often spends a whole day in the garden at weekends, even though a built-in sprinkler system waters all the plants, and irrigates the trees.

Left Imaginative stepping stones sculpted as mysterious smiling faces peer up amidst the lush ground-cover planting along the path to the left of the decking, and provide access to the plants when working in the garden. The plants include ajuga, tolmiea, and *Geranium rubescens*. The grassy foliage of *Hakonechloa macra* 'Aureola' is just visible in the bottom left-hand corner.

Right The view across the patio shows the open-air barbecue with plants in containers. Wooden decking to the right leads to a flight of steps which in turn leads up to an aerial dining space on an upper deck. The painted pergola, smothered in climbers, is to the right. The success of the garden depends on calculated plant chaos of a high order.

THE STRUCTURE

The garden measures 9 x 13 m/30 x 42 ft and depends for its effect on the contrast between an angular modern use of concrete and wood and the plethora of plants which encroach on to the hard surfaces. The built structure comprises a series of ascending rectangles – a patio and a lower and upper deck – and it is these changes of level that make the garden exciting, providing different spaces for alfresco living, and enabling the plants to be enjoyed from various angles. The planting also provides screening: by placing the built elements at the heart of the garden, privacy is ensured.

PAVING

The exposed aggregate concrete pavers form the most prosaic feature of the scheme, but were deliberately chosen by the designer as a neutral foil for the exuberant planting. Pavers like these are inexpensive, but stone, reconstituted stone, or brick would be an attractive alternative.

__ DECKING

Wooden decking makes a warm and agreeable surface to walk on and the formal use of natural materials combines well with the luxuriant planting. Constructing one area of decking at a higher level than the other has ingeniously provided a storage space below the platform. It is also a cheaper, easier way to achieve another level sitting area than excavating and terracing a sloping site. The woodwork must be professionally constructed from seasoned timber.

__ FOUNTAIN

Behind the pergola is a trickle fountain of stone backed by a reflecting mirror that gives this part of the garden an atmosphere of mysterious depth, as well as the gently lulling sound of running water.

__ PAINTED WOODWORK

(above) Colour in this garden comes not only from the plants but also from the built structure. The wood of the house itself and that of the structures in the garden is painted off-white, blue-grey and lilac, linking house and garden into one unit – something that is rarely done. Far from detracting from the plants, as a stark white might do, these hues enhance the scene.

Shades of grey-green to deep green would be another satisfactory colour scheme. The simple wooden pergola that spans the middle section of the garden rises to an apex in the centre, echoing the shape of the fretwork pediment of the balcony of the house. Painted wood does have serious maintenance implications. Unlike stained and treated wood that continues to look natural as it weathers and fades in the sun, or gathers lichens in cool and damp, painted wood relies on looking pristine for its full effect. To disentangle the plants from their supports and to rub down and repaint the wood in this garden would be a daunting task – but for those to whom their garden is all-important, it would be worth the effort. Like all wooden structures out-of-doors, these elements will need periodic checks for rot.

Above A close-up of just a few of the plants at the eastern edge of the patio shows how variety of habit, leaf-shape and colour have been considered in the placing. The striking purple foliage of *Phormium* 'Dark Delight' dominates the group. *Fuchsia excorticata purpurescens* behind it echoes its reddish leaf tones, while the narrow arching leaves of *Cortaderia selloana* 'Sunstripe' and *Spiraea japonica* 'Gold Flame' in the foreground provide clear colour contrast.

THE PLANTING

This plant-collector's garden has about 150 trees, shrubs, climbers, grasses, perennials and other plants crammed into the minute area, and the owner keeps adding new plants in spite of the shortage of space. Plants in pots form drifts along the edges of the paving and decking, and colonize the tables and barbecue. Every corner of this garden offers an interesting composition of forms, textures and colours. The mild winters make it possible to exploit the dramatic silhouettes of members of the palm family such as trachycarpus, chamaerops and the palm-like cordylines, as well as the tall tree ferns dicksonia and cyathea. The grassy, spiky theme is sustained at a lower level with plants like hakonechloa and cortaderia, as well as phormiums and yuccas. Plenty of plants with softer outlines provide a foil to these bold leaf forms. Another characteristic of the garden's planting is the extensive use of foliage colours – particularly golds and reddish-bronzes – which provide a rich context for the many orange, red and pink-toned flowers that thrive here.

Watering is built-in, but fertilizing is done annually by hand. The main regular tasks are those of tidying and neatening the plants – removing dead flower heads and damaged leaves. Plants also need periodic thinning and pruning. To accommodate such concentrated planting, radical pruning of the trees and larger shrubs is essential. This is a major task, but it does allow the wonderful profusion of choice plants to be grown in such a small area. The fact that few of the plants are deciduous means that the garden retains plenty of year-round structure. This also makes maintenance a perennial task. Instead of the single major blitz at the end of the growing season faced by gardeners in temperate climates – sweeping up leaves, removing dead stems, and sometimes lifting and dividing, after which both garden and gardener enjoy a relatively restful period – these plants need keeping in good trim all the year.

POOL BED

Two fan-like palms dominate the bed by the pool near the house.
1 Chusan (*Trachycarpus fortunei*), which has sprays of creamy flowers.
2 A dwarf fan palm (*Chamaerops humilis*).
3 Shrubs in the bed include gold-leaved *Spiraea japonica* 'Goldflame' and *Lonicera nitida* 'Baggesen's Gold'.
4 *Polygala* x *dalmaisiana*.
5 Apple 'MacIntosh Red' is espaliered on the house wall below the balcony.

Below Like many abutilons 'Souvenir de Bonn' is fast-growing and has a long flowering period.

EAST BED

Along the wall is a collection of choice trees and shrubs.

6 *Lycianthes rantonnei.*

7 *Magnolia* x *soulangeana.*

8 *Acer pseudoplatanus* 'Prinz Handjery'.

9 In front, among other shrubs, are the stiff spikes of *Cordyline australis* 'Albertii'.

10 *Cortaderia selloana* 'Sunstripe'.

11 *Phormium* 'Dark Delight'.

12 *Fuchsia excorticata purpurescens* sustains the theme of bronze foliage and red flowers.

13 *Prunus cerasifera* 'Pissardii'.

14 *Podocarpus gracilior.*

15 *Brahea edulis.*

16 *Acer palmatum.*

17 *Justicia carnea.*

STEPPING STONES

18 Planting around the path suits ground-hugging shade-tolerant plants such as ajugas, *Tolmiea menziesii* 'Taff's Gold' and hardy cranesbill geraniums, including *G. rubescens*. A variegated toad-lily, *Tricyrtis hirta* 'Variegata', relishes the shady site, and farther along grassy-leaved lilyturf (*Liriope muscari variegata*) provides ground cover beside the stones. Virtually all of these are invasive spreaders and demand regular and ruthless reduction.

SOUTH BOUNDARY

19 A large escallonia stands at the centre iflanked by two tree ferns.

20 *Cyathea cooperi.*

21 *Dicksonia antarctica.* The boundary at the rear of the plot is screened by ivy.

PERGOLA

22 Climbers including pink *Clematis montana, Rosa* 'New Dawn' and white-flowered *Jasminum polyanthum* assure a succession of seasonal interest.

PERGOLA SHADE

23 The pergola's canopy deepens the shade in the south-west corner, creating almost woodland conditions. Moist, deep, acidic soil suits a range of shrubs like azaleas and rhododendrons, *Cleyera japonica* "Tricolor" hydrangeas, as well as perennials such as alpinia, hedychium and carex.

24 Houttuynia grows around the trickle fountain.

WEST BORDER

25 Behind the seat is a galaxy of colourful flowering shrubs, from camellias in spring, through rhododendrons and *Cestrum elegans* to a summer-long display including roses, fuchsias, the Chilean firebush (*Embothrium coccineum*)

and *Brugmansia* 'Charles Grimaldi'. Abutilons making a special feature in this bed are 'Souvenir de Bonn', 'Tangerine' and 'Mariane'.

CONTAINER PLANTING

Clusters of pots make ad-hoc plant compositions on the edges of the decks, around the paved area, on the tables and even on the barbecue where cacti and succulents from indoors are spending a summer break. Most of these will outgrow their containers and most require regular repotting in fresh compost to sustain their vigour.

A DECORATIVE POTAGER

The decorative but productive kitchen garden is one of the most ambitious of all forms of garden art. It depends for its effect upon firm geometric structure. In the summer months it should be a cornucopia held in place by formally clipped evergreens, prettily paved paths and trained fruit trees. Even in the depths of winter it should be a place to admire: the skilful gardener would take care to see that during these cold months the potager was enlivened with well-sited cabbages, leeks, parsnips, celeriac, Brussels sprouts as well as frost-resistant salad greens. Moreover, vegetables call for rotation and particular soil conditions so that every year there is the challenge of making a new plan, re-siting the crops not only to produce their annual yield but delight the eye in a different way by thoughtful and surprising juxtapositions of leaf shape, texture and colour.

This Dutch potager is a masterpiece of the genre but a very accessible one. Its structure calls for simple inexpensive materials: a geometric arrangement of brick paths with a modest sundial as a focal point. The enclosing hedges would demand patience as they grew, so too might the topiary and fruit trees unless they were bought in fully trained. Otherwise, as not only most vegetables are annuals, but also many salad crops mature within a few weeks, the effect could be virtually instantaneous.

To maintain the effect demands a great deal of work. To keep a succession of crops in the beds is a challenge in itself; to keep them looking good needs constant vigilance. But the end result would reward you with the creation of one of the most difficult of all garden pictures, and give you the satisfaction of consuming fresh produce all the year.

Right The view from the herb garden shows how the well-defined clean paths make a strong ground-level pattern. The permanent verticals are provided by the clipped box and trained apple trees. To the left the potager is firmly held in and protected with a rich dark green yew hedge through which mophead plane trees have been trained. In winter, this makes a dramatic contrast with the other hedges which are of hornbeam that turns russet.

Left A terracotta pot on a pedestal, here arising above cabbages and potatoes, is a focal point in one of the spandrel gardens. It is strikingly planted with one of the marrow family to give both architectural leaves and edible produce. It would need watering daily, but the delightful effect is well worth the effort. To the left is one of the standard gooseberries.

CENTRAL FOCAL POINT (*left*) The view along the main path that bisects the garden looks towards one of the gates framed by a hornbeam hedge and arch. The sundial in the centre of the garden is encircled by bronze lettuces, (which have been allowed to bolt), cabbages and rhubarb which, by mid-summer almost cover the path. *Lavandula angustifolia* 'Hidcote' and standard 'Iceberg' roses mark the entrances to each of the four gardens-within-the-garden. The central sundial holds the whole composition together, but its place could be taken by a large pot, a fountain or well-head or alternatively, a symmetrically trained specimen tree, or a topiary piece such as a box cakestand or a bay obelisk. Box provides multiple evergreen accents, which anchor the design; while vertical accents are made by symmetrically sited trained apple and pear trees and standard roses.

THE STRUCTURE

The garden is about 15 m/50 ft. square It is surrounded by hedges, with picket gates for access at either end of the cross axis path. The design brings home the importance of strong articulation at ground level in the laying out of any potager. By quartering it, four separate areas are created, the one in the sunniest corner given to herbs framed by beds of strawberries. The other three incorporate some fruit trees and bushes but are basically assigned to a rotation of crops. In this design virtually nothing but straight lines has been used but an equally balanced composition could be achieved using curves, ovals and circles. The important point is to use the hard-surface elements, hedges and vertical accents, like the topiary and fruit trees, to establish overall balance and order. Each of the four spandrels is a composition in itself. Great attention has been paid to all the vistas created by the main paths: each terminates in a seat, a gate or some other focal point. What is ostensibly missing from this potager are some of the essential services; this is because they are sited outside its boundaries. If this was your only garden, or you had no room elsewhere to put them, there is no reason why they could not be incorporated within the main scheme. A well designed garden shed covered in climbers would make a good culmination to one of the vistas; equally, a small greenhouse could become the main feature of one of the quarters, perhaps balanced by a fruit cage in another quarter. A cold frame or two could easily be incorporated into one of the borders. A vegetable garden needs the constant enrichment of its soil, so you will need an area for manure and the making of compost. And you may need space for burning debris.

PATHS

Paths provide working access so must be wide enough for a gardener with a wheelbarrow. Here the paths make effective use of brick, which is suitable for the workman-like, practical ethos of a potager, and also unifies the design. The main paths are given emphasis by being slightly wider than the others, and the way the bricks are aligned, especially at path crossings, helps to guide the eye and articulate the design. Paths must be either hand-weeded or painted annually with weedkiller. You would certainly want to avoid sprays in such proximity to edible plants.

BEDS

Most are small enough to tend easily by reaching in from either side. (It may be useful to introduce stepping stones to the larger ones). Using old railway sleepers or containing coping to edge the beds would raise the soil level a little and so ensure that it did not become waterlogged, and would also help to stop soil spilling on to the paths.

BOUNDARIES

Most fruit and vegetables call for protection from the elements and the creation of a micro-climate. Here yew and hornbeam hedges make the enclosure. Although handsome, they do have disadvantages: they not only cast shade but suck food and water away from the produce unless their roots are contained, for instance, by sinking tough plastic corrugated sheeting to hold them in. Walls and various forms of fencing would be an alternative – and instant – solution; they also offer the attraction of being a surface able to support espaliered fruit and climbers. Many productive gardens also need protection from wildlife, and pest-proof wire netting may have to be incorporated.

THE PLANTING

The structural planting includes the fruit trees, roses and punctuating box bushes. Other permanent plants are the fruit bushes (standard gooseberries and raspberries) and strawberry plants. Apart from perennials in the herb garden, which call for periodic division and re-planting, all the remaining beds are given over to rotation of crops. Many kinds of vegetable are grown and there are not only annual changes but variation from month

vegetables. The first includes legumes and salads which call for freshly manured ground. The second includes root crops that flourish in soil manured the previous season, but also need a fresh dressing of general-purpose fertilizer such as bonemeal. The third includes brassicas which also require fertilizer as well as an additional dressing of lime. The beds are then rotated in sequence to ensure that the ground is not depleted, as each group takes out certain nutrients

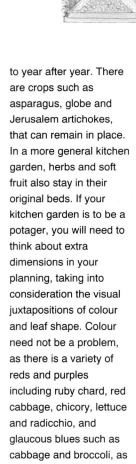

Above Chives (*Allium schoenoprasum)* add tangy relish to salads and, if allowed to flower, make pretty edging.

to month, with catch-crops taking advantage of space between slower-growing immature plants. A vegetable garden is traditionally divided into beds according to the cultivation demands of three main groups of

from the soil. Ideally the beds should be arranged on a north-south axis so that both sides receive equal measures of sun. It is essential to draw up a master plan indicating the three-year cycle of each bed that can be referred

to year after year. There are crops such as asparagus, globe and Jerusalem artichokes, that can remain in place. In a more general kitchen garden, herbs and soft fruit also stay in their original beds. If your kitchen garden is to be a potager, you will need to think about extra dimensions in your planning, taking into consideration the visual juxtapositions of colour and leaf shape. Colour need not be a problem, as there is a variety of reds and purples including ruby chard, red cabbage, chicory, lettuce and radicchio, and glaucous blues such as cabbage and broccoli, as well as the wide range of greens. Oriental salad

greens include bright flowers and nasturtiums (*Tropaeolum majus)*, which will climb as well as sprawl, and have edible flowers and leaves. Vegetables that climb, such as runner beans, can add strong vertical accents if they are trained up cane supports ranked in seried rows or arranged in wigwams. Marrows or squashes can also be grown up trellis or more elaborate arches. Other pretty effects can be achieved though the use of reproduction antique pottery cloches.

CENTRAL PATH

1 Red lettuce and purple-blue cabbage.
2 Rhubarb.
3 *Lavandula* 'Hidcote' surrounds two groups of

four white standard 'Iceberg' roses. These mark the entrances into the four main quadrants.

HERB GARDEN

4 A wide range is grown in this garden: rue (*Ruta graveolens)*, thyme (*Thymus vulgaris)*, anise (*Pimpinella anisum)*, sage (*Salvia officinalis)*, marjoram (*Origanum vulgare)*, basil (*Ocimum basilicum)*, borage (*Borago officinalis)*, fennel (*Foeniculum vulgare)*, parsley (*Petroselinum crispum)*, French tarragon (*Artemisia dracunculus)* and mint (*Mentha)*. Rosemary (*Rosmarinus officinalis)* is grown in a pot and wintered indoors. There is a very large number of herbs, but growing those most

commonly used in cooking would narrow the list down considerably.

VEGETABLES
5 Legumes and salad crops.
6 Runner beans on cane wigwams.
7 Spinach.
8 Brassicas.
9 Courgettes (zucchini) grow in a pot.
10 Potatoes.

SOFT FRUIT
11 Strawberries.
12 Blackcurrants.
13 Raspberries and redcurrants.

TRAINED FRUIT
Well trained fruit trees provide both decorative structure and produce, and this garden makes exemplary use of many forms. When planning to grow fruit, go to a good nurseryman for advice on the appropriate choice for your area, on root stocks suited to the space available and on compatible varieties for cross pollination. Many fruit tree growers can now supply ready-trained trees and bushes.
14 Standard gooseberries mark the four corners of

Above Small trained apple trees contribute spring blossom and summer fruit and also form valuable living structure.

the brassica bed.
15 Two pairs of dwarf apple trees trained as aerial goblets.

16 Espaliered pear trees line the path.
17 Arbour of espaliered pear trees.

Below The view down the cross-axis path looks towards the pear arbour that frames a double iron seat. The apple trees, trained as goblets, stand as sentinels to the vista. Just in front of them are two terracotta jars used to blanch produce such as rhubarb or celery, while behind them rise the outsize leaves of rhubarb.

Left The view across the front garden to the path from the entrance gate. A handsome *Acer palmatum* 'Butterfly' rises above the lantern, and a planting of shrubs and ferns. A carefully sculpted *Nothofagus antarctica* stands at the corner of the house, and fine white gravel, symbolizing the stream of life, ties the different elements together.

Right The vista from half way down the tiny back garden, where the wall of clipped thuja frames an exquisite composition of manicured evergreens, small flowering shrubs and trees set amidst rocks, ferns and moss.

A JAPANESE GARDEN

This remarkable garden has been created over a period of twenty years. It is a passionate attempt to recreate an authentic Japanese garden. Few will wish to emulate this extraordinary and exacting achievement, but it provides inspiration in terms of style, design and planting, and provides an object lesson on the handling of small spaces. Japanese garden tradition consists of miniaturizing and formalizing the essence of natural landscape in a highly sophisticated and symbolic way.

The evolution of the Japanese garden has taken many centuries. Unlike our modern gardens in the western world, Japanese gardens are imbued with an esoteric network of allusions and symbols, all readily understood by the garden visitor. Each garden, however small, embraces a complex series of pictures that evoke mountains and valleys, rivers, lakes or the sea. To interpret these scenes in the way that the Japanese would do so requires intensive study of Japanese garden art and philosophy. Where we see a group of stones placed with aesthetic precision, the Japanese will not only see a whole mountain range, but each stone as a spiritual symbol.

To make a garden exactly like the one that is included here is an aspiration for only the most dedicated, though a richly rewarding one, but the garden still contains many achievable ideas.

ENTRANCE (*left*)
A path leads from the entrance arch or chuman. Traditional Japanese stepping stones are incorporated into the setts, and bamboo is used for the fencing and gate grille.

THE STRUCTURE

These two gardens, in a site that measures 18 x 7 m\60 x 22ft overall at the front and back of a semi-detached house in a village in Holland, are each based on a specific category of Japanese garden. The front garden was inspired by a monastery garden in the hills near Kyoto, and includes features such as a stone slab bridge over a meandering stream of white gravel and a bamboo water-operated deer scare. At the back is a traditional tea garden where a paved area overlooks a pond fed by a waterfall and a miniature landscape of stones, moss, trees, shrubs and ferns.

DEER SCARE

A traditional deer scare inside a bamboo lattice fence in the front garden was originally used to scare off wild boar and deer from crops. Water runs through a thin bamboo pipe into a thicker length of bamboo with a hollowed-out chamber, and as the water empties, the pipe falls back, hitting a rock with a sharp clack. This never-ending movement and sound suggests the process and effects of time on the unchanging elements in the garden.

LANTERNS

Japanese lanterns have complex symbolic associations, though their prime purpose is to illuminate. In the front garden, two lanterns – a snow-viewing lantern and a buried lantern – are sited to light the way to the front door. In the back garden, two light the way to the tea house, and a third is placed near the pond to create reflections. Imported lanterns like these are sometimes available.

WATERFALL

To the Japanese, a waterfall is symbolic of the source of life. It should convey the impression of falling from a stream in a valley behind; it must be sited where sun and moonlight falling on it can be appreciated; and it must have a basin of rocks through and into which the water can plunge, symbolizing the obstacles that everyone has to overcome in their lifetime. With modern electrically powered pumps the construction of a feature like this would pose few problems, but it is essential that the water is kept clean and clear so that it can reflect the surrounding plants.

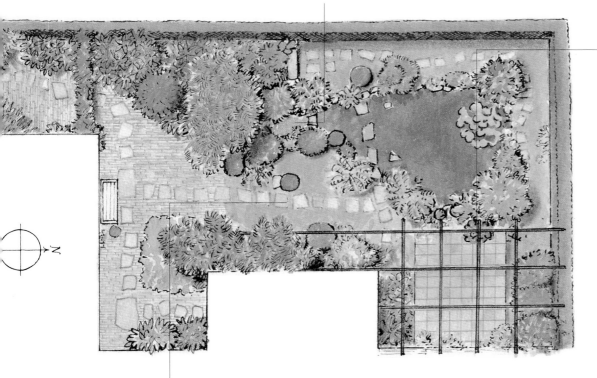

TEA HOUSE OR CHESAKI

The tea ceremony, an elaborate ritual designed to instill the virtues of modesty, politeness, restraint and sensibility, has an important role in Japanese life, and a tea house has a correspondingly important place in the garden. Here it is simply constructed of a canopy of beams over a paved area, but it commands the key garden picture – the pond and waterfall. A Japanese tea house will contain one spray of flowers in a vase, and the status and attention accorded to that spray explains the virtual absence of flowers that might detract from it in the garden itself. A water spout for ceremonial hand-washing before the tea ceremony stands beside a garden shed disguised by a covering of bamboo matting.

STONES AND STEPPING STONES

Stones are essential elements in a Japanese garden, where each one is carefully chosen and imbued with meaning. For aesthetic reasons, they are placed with studied irregularity, but they are also used to direct visitors through the garden so that they may appreciate its every detail. Stepping stones lead from the house to the pergola – a passage to self-illumination.

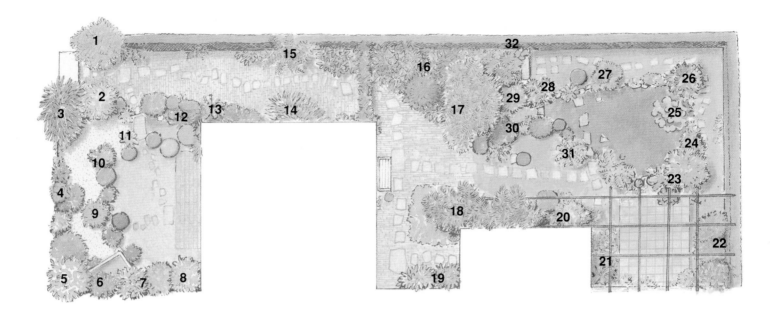

THE PLANTING

Japanese planting is based on religious belief rooted first in Shintoism and later in Buddhism; both hold nature in the deepest reverence. The aim once again is the symbolic representation of elements found in nature, and anyone attempting to make a Japanese garden should try to understand the complexities of choice, siting and cultivation of plants. Not only must every plant be in a position that corresponds to its native habitat, but a balanced composition must also be achieved.

Plants will include deciduous trees and shrubs such as cherries, magnolias, azaleas and rhododendrons. Gravel, stone, sagina moss and ferns are used to link the planted elements together. Attention is paid to subtle gradations of colour through the year, and deciduous trees are chosen for their all-year-round beauty, their branch formation, bark texture, leaf shape and changing colour through the seasons.

Anyone embarking on a full-scale Japanese

Below Magnolia stellata slowly forms a dense bushy shrub whose fragrant spring flowers precede the leaves.

garden would first have to make a prolonged study of Japanese garden philosophy and horticultural practices, including a ruthless and highly sophisticated approach to pruning.

FRONT AND SIDE GARDENS
1 A flowering cherry.
2 *Acer palmatum* 'Butterfly'.
3 *Sinarundinaria murieliae*.
4 Ranged along the front border are *Ilex crenata* 'Convexa', *Pinus pumila* 'Nana' and *Osmanthus heterophyllus*.
5 *Styrax japonicus*.
6 *Ilex crenata* 'Convexa'.
7 Around the deer scare are *Osmanthus heterophyllus*, *Magnolia stellata* 'Royal Star' and *Pieris japonica* 'Prelude'.

8 *Prunus strobus*.
9 *Acer palmatum* 'Garnet'.
10 A group of *Buxus sempervirens* 'Suffruticosa', Japanese azaleas and *Osmanthus heterophyllus*.
11 Ferns and ophiopogon are tucked in near the stone bridge.
12 Grouped near the corner of the house are *Buxus sempervirens* 'Suffruticosa', *Rhododendron kiusianum* 'Album', *Pinus pumila* 'Nana' and *Pieris japonica* 'Prelude'.
13 *Nothofagus antarctica*.
14 Flowering cherry.
15 *Dryopteris erythrosora*.

BACK GARDEN
16 A group of rhododendrons.
17 *Rhus glabra*.
18 *Osmanthus heterophyllus* grows beneath a mature *Wisteria*

Right This view from the waterfall end of the pond shows the concentrated but carefully placed planting of acers, pieris, azaleas and ferns among the rocks, stones and moss. The pine on the left, a *sine qua non* of every Japanese garden, symbolizes the dignity of the masculine power of longevity.

sinensis 'Alba'.
19 *Magnolia liliiflora* 'Nigra' and rhododendrons.
20 Rhododendrons and ferns.
21 *Acer tataricum ginnala*.
22 A mixed planting of hostas and ferns.
23 A group of pink, white and mauve-flowering Japanese azaleas.
24 *Acer palmatum atropurpureum*.
25 Waterlilies grow in the pool.
26 *Ginkgo biloba*.
27 *Pinus*.
28 *Pieris japonica*.
29 *Acer palmatum dissectum* 'Dissectum Ornatum'.
30 Juniper, pine and rhododendron.
31 *Dryopteris erythrosora*.
32 Clipped thuja hedge.

Right Looking down on the garden gives a vivid impression of the prolific use of climbers and evergreens to make up for the absence of trees and a lawn. The circular pergola around the pond creates the effect of a room within a room and forms a shady cloister in which to sit on sunny days.

Opposite Around the small circular pond there are in the main moisture-loving plants including purple loosestrife (*Lythrum salicaria* 'Robert'), the umbrella plant (*Darmera peltata*) and *Iris sibirica*. A simple container terminates the vista and is framed by an arch covered in climbers.

AN URBAN BOWER

This small courtyard garden brilliantly solves many of the common problems which arise in urban garden-making at the same time as creating a habitat for a stunning array of plants. Its strong ground pattern goes back to the earliest renaissance garden plans, a square or rectangle divided into four quarters with a circle at the centre. There is no room for large trees, but the designer, K.T. Noordhuis, has handsomely met the need for height with a circular pergola enclosing the pond area, an arch, pleached limes as aerial boundary screening, and an abundance of climbers that double the bloom potential of the garden. This defined structure is host to a rich array of both shade-tolerant and sun-loving plants. The basic design is so strong that the planting could be accommodated to any level of commitment: here the scheme is the proud creation of avid gardeners who enjoy spending time tending it, but, with simplification, the format would make a superb low-maintenance town garden.

THE STRUCTURE

This is a classic formula adaptable to many sites: an irregular space, roughly 10 x 10 m (32 x 32 ft), has been given a deceptive symmetry by the superimposition of what is almost a square divided into four spandrels. By jamming the formal garden rectangle against two boundary walls, space has been released to make terraces setting off

the two façades of the back of the house. Each view across the garden and the central pond terminates in its own special feature: a garden seat, a wall-fountain, a table for dining alfresco and a wall-fountain. Care has also been taken that the cross-axes relate to the architecture of the house, in one case a window and in the other a space between two windows.

AERIAL HEDGING

Pleached lime trees whose branches have been trained along horizontal bamboos make perfect aerial hedging, which is a wonderful means of

securing privacy, or screening out unsightly views. The trees will call for an annual winter prune, ruthlessly cutting off all offending branches and twigs, and careful tying in.

PERGOLA

The central cloister pergola is a custom-built but simple cast-iron structure. It creates a circular central room furnished with four symmetrically arranged black-painted curved wooden benches.

WATER FEATURES (*left*)

The circular pond is the garden's focal point and the water acts as a mirror reflecting light into the courtyard. The coping is of a kind that is available in reconstituted stone. The water is pumped around a circuit via a rivulet to the elaborate wall-fountain. The pump also oxygenates the water. As the fountain – a stylized bird on a column – is only the barest trickle, the water in the pond remains virtually undisturbed and so therefore it is possible to grow water lilies and marginals.

ARCHES AND PILLARS
Cast-iron arches preside over three of the entrances to the central paths, each framing a viewpoint. These and the wire-mesh pillars provide support for climbers. Painted or stained wood may be less durable and require more maintenance but would be an attractive, cheaper alternative.

BOX HEDGING
Low evergreen box hedging defines the ground pattern and holds in the spandrel flowerbeds. Other possibilities, though less satisfactory would be euonymus, *Lonicera nitida* or yew, although it would be difficult to keep them so low. All call for annual clipping, regular feeding and, from time to time, the severance of roots that have invaded the flowerbed.

PATHS
All the paths are covered in small shells laid over old tiles. The pale shells lighten the effect but make the courtyard appear bigger than it is. Gravel, stone or brick would be alternatives, but when making the choice, always take the materials of the house into consideration.

THE PLANTING

This is a beautifully and skilfully planted garden. Careful attention has been paid to every season. Planted so that they grow up between other plants, hundreds of small bulbs including *Anemone blanda*, chionodoxa, crocus, fritillaries, iris and narcissi and snowdrops flower in spring, followed by allium and lilies in summer and cyclamen and *Crocus sativus* in autumn. In particular it is a lesson in the use of climbers which add leaf and bloom for many seasons and virtually double the ground-level planting. The climbers involve a major labour commitment: they need annual pruning, training and tying-in to ensure that they are contained. The plants in the beds also call for pruning, cutting down, staking and general attention. Each bed is intensively cultivated, so constant enrichment of the soil is essential. To reduce the work load, it would be possible to simplify the planting by choosing climbers that require minimal pruning, and fill the spandrel beds with ground-cover perennials, putting a strong evergreen vertical accent such as a clipped juniper or a sculptural feature such as a puttio to represent each of the seasons at the centre of each bed.

1 The four spandrel beds are enclosed by dwarf box

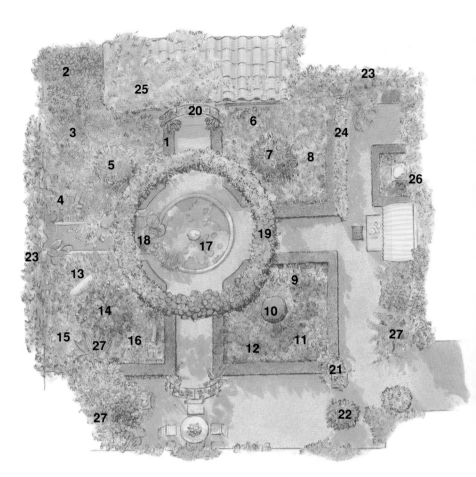

Below Epimedium x *rubrum* is excellent evergreen ground cover that tolerates sun or shade.

hedging (*Buxus sempervirens* 'Suffruticosa').

SOUTH SPANDREL BED
2 *Hedera helix* clambers up the shady walls.
3 *Skimmia japonica* and *Pieris japonica* are surrounded by *Primula beesiana, P. bulleyana* and *P. florindae*.
4 Ivy-leaved toadflax, greater celandine and red Mollis azaleas.
5 *Caragana arborescens* 'Pendula' makes a strong vertical feature in the middle of the bed.

WEST SPANDREL BED
6 *Lamium orvala*, epimedium, *Cornus sericea* and ferns including *Matteuccia struthiopteris*.
7 *Paeonia suffruticosa*.
8 *Helleborus viridis, H. niger* and codonopsis.

NORTH SPANDREL BED
9 Vinca, hosta, campanula and sedum.
10 *Ligustrum ovalifolium* 'Aureum' is trained as a mophead.
11 *Viola riviniana*

Purpurea Group, *V. sororia* and cleomes.
12 Mahonia and *Tiarella cordifolia*.

EAST SPANDREL BED
13 Ferns, Soloman's seal, figwort (*Scrophularia*) and marsh marigolds (*Caltha palustris*) make the most of the shade and moisture near the wall fountain.
14 *Rosa* 'Red Dorothy Perkins' on a support makes the vertical centrepiece.
14 Several varieties of *Ajuga reptans* make good

ground-cover.
15 Hostas.
16 *Symphytum ibericum.*

POND
17 Small waterlilies are
planted in the pond.
18 Nearby are the
umbrella plant (*Darmera
peltatua*), *Lythrum
salicaria* 'Robert', *Salix
helvetica, Bergenia
cordifolia, Iris sibirica* and
*Sisyrinchium
angustifolium.*

CIRCULAR PERGOLA
19 This is covered in a
mixture of evergreen and
flowering climbers
including scented
honeysuckle (*Lonicera
henryi* and *L. japonica*
'Halliana'), *Humulus
lupulus,* American
Bittersweets (*Celastrus
scandens* (f) and *C.s.*

'Hercules' (m)'), actinidia
hybrids (m and f), potato
vines (*Solanum
jasminoides* 'Album' and
S. dulcamara 'Variegatum').

ARCHES AND PILLARS
20 *Clematis tangutica, C.
tibetana vernayi* and
Hedera helix 'Goldheart'.
21 *Clematis vitalba.*
22 *Parthenocissus
quinquefolia.*

AERIAL HEDGING
23 Pleached lines (*Tilia
platyphyllos* 'Rubra') are
trained as an aerial scren
over the gate and flanking
the wall fountain. Against
each is planted a Viticella
hybrid clematis: 'Minuet',
'Little Nell' and 'Etoile
Violette'.
24 Fruiting red currants
and Japanese wine berry
are trained along a frame.

Below Fritillaria meleagris is a spring flowering bulb that is
best left to naturalize in shade.

ENCLOSING WALLS
25 *Clematis tangutica*
climbs over the tiled roof.
26 Each of the climbers
that clothe the walls has
been carefully selected
according to the aspect,
so that shady walls are
covered with *Hedera helix*
and *H. colchica* 'Dentata
Variegata', *Hygrangea
anomala petiolaris* ,
*Kadsura japonica,
Euonymus fortunei* 'Silver
Queen' and *Jasminum
nudiflorum.* Sunnier walls
are host to *Ceanothus* x
delileanus 'Gloire de

Versailles'. *Buddleja* 'Ile
de France', *Wisteria
sinensis, Campsis
radicans, Solanum
crispum* 'Glasnevin' *and
Passiflora caerulea.*
Among other climbers are
*Clematis alpina, C.
montana, C.* 'Mrs Robert
Brydon', *C.* 'Mrs
Cholmondeley' and *C.*
'Royal Velours'.

CONTAINERS
27 Ferns, agapanthus and
agaves can be moved to
suit their shade or sun
requirements.

Above Like all the beds,
the north spandrel is
densely planted. Beneath
the mophead ligustrum
are *Campanula carpatica,*
vinca, *Meconopsis
betonicifolia, Saxifraga
cortusifolia fortunei,*
sedum, mahonia and
Tiarella cordifolia.

A SIX-STAGE GARDEN

This ambitious and perfectly articulated narrow town garden marries a rich and abundant planting with an unerring sense of geometry. An understated terrace next to the house acts as a forecourt from which an enchantingly luxuriant vista progresses through another five contrasting garden experiences. Statues stand at the head of the steps, and from here lavishly planted mixed borders lead to a formal enclosure where symmetrical planting bordered by box hedging surrounds a stone vase on a pedestal. A second pair of borders follow, and then comes the climax: a rose and herb garden of geometric simplicity, enclosed by a beech hedge and presided over by an arbour spangled with roses and clematis, with a statue embowered within. A final coda introduces a simple summerhouse with a marble pillared entrance, reached by a small bridge separating two lily ponds.

This plant-lover's paradise is crammed with some two hundred trees, shrubs, climbers, roses and herbaceous perennials, as well as having box and beech hedging; even waterlilies find a place. All this requires a dedicated horticultural commitment to ensure that the garden is in top condition at all times of the year. However, the whole area is paved, so there is no mowing, and the strong structure containing the plants means that a complex garden such as this could be kept in perfect order by someone working the equivalent of one afternoon a week throughout the year.

Statues of Ceres and Pomona frame the garden's central axis, emphasizing the strong architectural framework. Foliage, particularly of hosta, astilbe, ferns and box hedging breaks the line of the brick paving, and the eye is led past the vase to the rose garden with its central statue.

THE STRUCTURE

In this long narrow site of about 6 x 33m \20 x 110ft, the controlling element is the central axis which widens and narrows to bind together a succession of contrasting gardens. The different areas change from open to closed and from informal to formal, with the planting in different colour schemes reflecting these changes. The result is that the garden seems bigger than it actually is. A plan of this kind offers endless possibilities of adaption – rearranging the sequence according to the space

CENTRAL VISTA (*left*)
The view from the summerhouse at the far end of the garden leads past clipped box balls on the marble bridge and the stately foliage of *Rheum palmatum* to the rose and herb garden. Standard 'Iceberg' roses frame a statue beneath an arbour covered in a tumbling canopy of *Rosa* 'Félicité Perpétue' and climbing *R.* 'Souvenir de la Malmaison'.

PONDS (*right*)
Water spouts into troughs that overflow into the lily pools, adding movement and sound to the composition. Small central water jets would be an alternative way of achieving this.

ROSE AND HERB
GARDEN
This garden is formed of
squares within a perfect
square. An arched iron
frame rising from the
four corners of the
central bed forms a
canopy smothered in
climbing roses and
clematis, and provides

shelter for a statue. A
similar structure could
also be made of painted
wood and trellis or even,
though less attractively,
of plasticized metal alloy.
Rails make delightful
and unexpected frames
for the herb beds, each
planted with a standard
rose.

VASE GARDEN
A formal interlude
between the two pairs of
long borders, the
planting is structural and
repetitive. Behind a
rectangle defined by a
low clipped hedge of
Buxus sempervirens and

B.s. 'Latifolia Maculata'
is a mirror planting of
clipped weeping purple
beech alternating with
box cubes and
underplanted with ferns.
The vase overflows with
helichrysum, verbena
and glechoma.

PAVING
The frost-resistant bricks
are inexpensive, durable,
and easily swept. Their
small size makes the
garden appear larger than
it is, and their uniformity
provides good foil to the
luxurious planting.

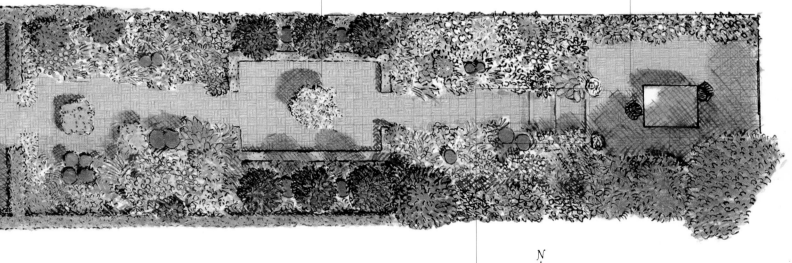

N

ORNAMENTS
The flanking statues on
the terrace make a
stunning entrance to the
garden, just as the
marble pillared archway
does at the far end: but
neither is essential to the
overall design. The
beautiful stone vase on
its pedestal, on the other

hand, and the arbour in
the rose garden, are
essential ingredients of
the garden plan. Of
course, alternative
objects could be used,
and there are plenty of
well-designed garden
ornaments in terracotta
or reconstituted stone on
the market today.

THE PLANTING

Most of the planting is concentrated in the two parallel but irregularly indented borders that run virtually the entire length of the garden. Colour schemes are carefully planned, and many plants are chosen for their foliage.

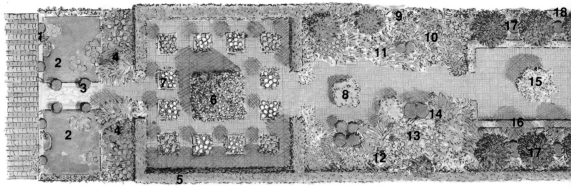

WATER GARDEN

1 *Wisteria sinensis* 'Alba' and *Rosa* 'Veilchenblau' are trained along the front of the summerhouse.
2 The pools contain red *Nymphaea* Hybrids.
3 The bridge is punctuated by box clipped balls in pots.
4 The two beds have mirror-image plantings of *Foeniculum vulgare* 'Purpureum', *Artemisia schmidtiana*, *Rheum palmatum*, *Hydrangea arborescens* 'Annabelle', *Heuchera* 'Pluie de Feu' *Asplenium scolopendrium*, and *Alchemilla mollis*.

ROSE AND HERB GARDEN

5 A hedge of *Fagus sylvatica* encloses the area.
6 A low inner and outer hedge of *Buxus sempervirens*, infilled with blue *Iris germanica*, contains the arbour which supports *Rosa* 'Félicité Perpétue', *R*. 'Climbing Wedding Day', *R*. 'Souvenir de la Malmaison', *Clematis* 'Pink Fantasy', *C*. 'Etoile Violette', and the white, repeat-flowering Bourbon *Rosa* 'Boule de Neige'.
7 The twelve small square beds each contain a standard rose: the four corner beds *R*. 'Ice Fairy', and the rest 'Iceberg'. Each is underplanted with a different herb.

FIRST BORDER GARDEN

The south-facing bed concentrates on blues, lilacs, pinks and whites while the north-facing bed opposite has warmer creams, yellows and apricots offset by ferns and evergreens.
8 A container overflowing with *Alchemilla mollis*, and also *Primula veris*.

9 Larger shrubs and perennials give height at the back: purple and lilac *Syringa vulgaris*, white *Hibiscus syriacus*, *Hydrangea aspera sargentiana*, *Rosa glauca* (syn. *R. rubrifolia*) and *Salvia sclarea*.
10 In the middle ground are a blue *Hydrangea macrophylla*, *Aquilegia alpina*, *Viburnum opulus* 'Roseum', *Aconitum* 'Spark's Variety', a blue *Delphinium* hybrid, *Phlox paniculata* 'Amethyst', *Thalictrum rochebrunanum*, a standard *Rosa* 'Charles de Gaulle', *R*. 'Königin von Dänemark' and *Hosta seiboldiana* var. *elegans*.
11 Closer to the path are *Artemisia schmidtiana*, *Geranium* 'Johnson's Blue', *Iris sibirica* 'Caesar', *Hebe pinguifolia* 'Pagei', *Nepeta* x *faassenii*, *Pulmonaria angustifolia*, *Viola* 'Molly Sanderson', bearded iris 'Dusky Dancer', *Ajuga reptans* 'Atropurpurea', *Brunnera macrophylla*, *Veronica gentianoides*,

Left Looking over a bank of *Alchemilla mollis* and through the beech hedge to the rose and herb garden and its rose-bedecked arbour. Two neatly railed beds are filled with herbs beneath standard 'Iceberg' roses.

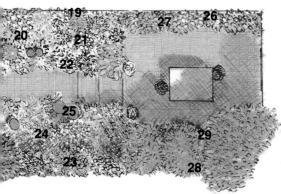

Viola odorata 'Alba', *Lavandula angustifolia*, *Viola odorata*, two clipped box balls, *Centaurea montana*, *Gypsophila paniculata* 'Bristol Fairy', *Salvia nemorosa* 'Mainacht', *Anchusa azurea* and *Rhododendron* 'Blue Tit'.
12 At the back of the north-facing bed, under the beech hedge, are *Corylus avellana*, *Matteuccia struthiopteris*, *Kirengeshoma palmata*, *Aruncus dioicus*, *Osmunda regalis*, *Ilex aquifolium* and *Scabiosa caucasica* 'Bressingham White'.
13 In the centre are two standard *Chamaecyparis*, *Ligularia przewalskii*, *Angelica archangelica* 'Sativa', two standard *Rosa* 'Dutch Gold', *Hydrangea quercifolia*, *Aconitum lamarckii*, an apricot *Azalea* Hybrid and *Hydrangea arborescens* 'Annabelle'.
14 In the foreground are *Artemisia schmidtiana*, *Lamium galeobdolon* 'Florentinum', *Euphorbia*

amygdaloides, *Hosta fortunei aureomarginata*, *Corydalis lutea*, two *Buxus sempervirens*, *Hemerocallis altissima*, *Hydrangea paniculata* 'Grandiflora', *Alchemilla mollis*, *Artemisia ludoviciana* 'Silver Queen', two standard *Chamaecyparis obtusa* 'Nana gracilis', *Hosta* 'Zounds', *H. fortunei* and *Hemerocallis* 'Carthage'.

VASE GARDEN
15 The vase is planted with *Helichrysum petiolare*, purple *Verbena* and *Glechoma hederacea* 'Variegata'.
16 Contained by a low mixed hedge of *Buxus sempervirens* and *B.s.* 'Latifolia Maculata', the two mirror-image borders in this garden introduce a dramatic change of colour and scale.
17 Each border contains three weeping *Fagus sylvatica* 'Purpurea Pendula', with clipped box cubes between, and underplanted with *Osmunda regalis*.

18 The climbers on the north wall are *Lonicera henryi* and *Clematis vitalba*.

SECOND BORDER GARDEN
19 Climbers on the wall behind this border are *Hedera helix* and *Clematis florida bicolor* 'Sieboldii'.
20 The south facing 'white' border has a background planting of *Osmunda regalis*, standard *Rosa* 'Iceberg' and *R.* 'White Dorothy', *Aruncus dioicus*, *Hydrangea paniculata* 'Grandiflora' and *Cornus kousa*.
21 In the middle ground are *Hydrangea arborescens* 'Annabelle', *Crambe cordifolia*, *Phlox paniculata* 'Fujiyama', a standard *Rosa* 'Iceberg' and *Rhododendron* 'Alice'.
22 In front of these, along the path, are *Hesperis matronalis*, two *Paeonia suffruticosa*, *Salvia argentea*, *Geranium richardsonii*, *Viola odorata*, *Astrantia major*, *Iris germanica*, *Hosta sieboldiana elegans*, *Crambe maritima*, *Rosa* 'Snow Carpet', a standard *Cotoneaster*, *Epimedium* x *youngianum* 'Yenomoto', *Cerastium tomentosum*, two clipped balls of *Buxus sempervirens*, *Anemone* x *hybrida* 'Honorine

Jobert', *Iris* 'Babyface', *Saponaria ocymoides*, *Artemisia ludoviciana*, a white *Azalea* Hybrid and *Filipendula purpurea alba*.
23 At the back of the north-facing border, which is dominated by strong pinks and whites are three *Rhododendron* Hybrids and *Syringa* x *chinensis*.

Below *Kirengeshoma palmata*, a shade-tolerant shrub, useful for its interesting foliage and late summer flowers.

24 In the middle ground are *Hydrangea macrophylla* 'Teller's Pink', *Phlox paniculata*, a standard *Ribes sanguineum*, two standard *Rosa* 'Sexy Rexy' and *Fuchsia magellanica* are interspersed with more *Osmunda regalis*.
25 In front are two bright pink *Azalea* Hybrids, *Sempervivum tectorum*, *Geranium macrorrhizum*, four clipped balls of *Buxus sempervirens*, *Anemone* x *hybrida* 'Königin Charlotte', a pink

Geranium, a pink *Paeonia* Hybrid, two *Dicentra formosa*, *Astilbe* 'Europa' and *Skimmia reevesiana*.

HOUSE TERRACE
26 The climbers on the south-facing wall include *Wisteria sinensis* that is trained on to the house, and three clematis – two

C. 'Capitaine Thuilleaux' and one *C.* 'Marie Boisselot' – as well as a *Jasminum nudiflorum* to flower in the winter.
27 At either end of the bed below are standard *Rosa* 'The Fairy', and in between, *Hydrangea macrophylla* is underplanted with *Primula veris*.
28 On the wall opposite are *Rosa filipes* 'Kiftsgate' and *Hedera helix*.
29 *Chamaecyparis pisifera* are planted for screening behind *Rhododendron* Hybrids.

INDEX

ACKNOWLEDGMENTS

The publisher thanks the photographers and organizations for their kind permission to reproduce the photographs on the following pages in this book:

Endpapers Vincent Motte; 1 Eric Crichton; 2-3 Garden Picture Library /Marijke Heuff; 5 Jerry Harpur; 6 Andrew Lawson; 7-8 Oman Productions Ltd; 9 Clive Nichols; 10 Andrew Lawson; 11 Oman Productions Ltd; 12-13 Architecture & Wohnen /Arwed Voss; 14 Brigitte Perdereau /designer Timothy Vaughan; 15 Marianne Majerus (sculpture by Alexander Relph); 16-17 Marijke Heuff (Mr & Mrs Voûte-van Heerde); 18 Lanny Provo /artist John Millan (John Cram/Kenilworth gardens, Asheville NC); 19 S&O Mathews; 20 Neil Campbell-Sharp; 21 Brigitte Perdereau /designer Timothy Vaughan; 22-23 Ianthe Ruthven (Georgie Walton); 25 Andrew Lawson; 26-27 Marijke Heuff (Margot Voorhoeve-van Suchtelen); 29 Marijke Heuff (Mr & Mrs Van Groeningen-Hazenberg); 31 Marijke Heuff (Mr & Mrs Van Groeningen-Hazenberg); 32-34 Brigitte Perdereau (François Catroux); 35 Andrew Lawson; 36-38 Jerry Harpur (Jacqui and Colin Small); 39 Clive Nichols; 40-41 Garden Picture Library /Henk Dijkman /designer Dick Beyer; 43 Andrew Lawson; 44-45 Elizabeth Whiting & Associates /Andreas von Einsiedel /designer Christopher Masson (Lee Wheeler); 47 S&O Mathews; 48-50 Garden Picture Library /Henk Dijkman /designer Mien Ruys; 51 S&O Mathews; 52-54 Neil Campbell-Sharp /designer Arabella Lenox-Boyd (Irène Beard); 55 Tania Midgley; 56-57 Marijke Heuff /designer Els Proost (Mr & Mrs Bakker-Mulder); 58 Andrew Lawson /designer Anthony Noel; 60 Christian Sarramon; 61 Marijke Heuff /designer Els Proost (Mr & Mrs Arends-Buying); 62 Jerry Harpur /Malcolm Hillier; 62-63 Ben Loftus /designer Ben Loftus (Carrie Hart); 64-65 Neil Campbell-Sharp (Mike & Wendy Perry); 66-68 Garden Picture Library /Ron Sutherland (Ann Mollo); 69 S&O Mathews; 70-74 Rob Gray /designer Adele Mitchell; 76-79 Jerry Harpur /designer Sonny Garcia (Genevieve di san Faustino); 80 above Jerry Harpur /designer Sonny Garcia (Genevieve di san Faustino); 80 below Andrew Lawson; 81 Photos Horticultural; 82-84 Jerry Harpur /designer Judith Sharpe (Liz and Nick Bliss); 86 left Tania Midgley; 86 right Photos Horticultural; 87 Jerry Harpur /designer Judith Sharpe (Liz and Nick Bliss); 88-92 Garden Picture Library /Steve Wooster /designer Henk Weijers; 93 Photos Horticultural; 94-97 George Lévêque /designer André van Wassenhove; 99 above Photos Horticultural; 99 below George Lévêque /designer André van Wassenhove; 100-101 George Lévêque (Mrs Etta de Haes, Middelburg); 102 Karen Bussolini; 103 Jerry Harpur (Lucy Gent); 104 Christian Sarramon; 105 Marijke Heuff /designer Liesbeth Sillem (Riny Blaisse); 106-107 Mick Hales /designer Dean Riddle; 108 Graeme Moore; 109 Marianne Majerus /designer Peter Aldington; 110-113 right Jerry Harpur /designer Sonny Garcia; 114 left Jerry Harpur /designer Sonny Garcia; 114 right Photos Horticultural; 116 Marijke Heuff (Ineke Greve); 117 George Lévêque (Ineke Greve); 118 Marijke Heuff (Ineke Greve); 120 Photos Horticultural; 121 above Eric Crichton; 121 below Marijke Heuff (Ineke Greve); 122-124 Garden Picture Library /Henk Dijkman (Geert Jansen); 126 Andrew Lawson; 127 Garden Picture Library /Henk Dijkman (Geert Jansen); 128-130 Garden Picture Library /Henk Dijkman /designer K T Noordhuis; 132 Photos Horticultural; 133 above Marijke Heuff /designer K T Noordhuis; 133 below Photos Horticultural; 134-138 Marijke Heuff (Pierre & Anne-Marie Feijen, Manu, Breda); 139 Garden Picture Library /Brian Carter.